P9-CMQ-065

PRAISE FOR
Core Knowledge Preschool

"I thought my child was learning a lot in her Core Knowledge preschool classroom, but I had no idea how much until, at the start of kindergarten, her teacher told me that not only had she passed the readiness test—she was at the top of her class!"

—*Parent of preschooler in Baltimore County Head Start, a Core Knowledge preschool*

"Core Knowledge preschoolers showed statistically significant improvement in language, literacy, math, and social skills . . . and continued to maintain this advantage through the early elementary grades."

—*Robert Bradley, Ph.D., University of Arkansas*

"The students entering kindergarten from the Core Knowledge preschool are standing out in our kindergarten classrooms. Their interest in reading is the most noticeable characteristic. They are reading or ready to read when they enter kindergarten. . . . Their math skills and conceptual understanding are above the rest. . . . Our kindergarten teachers are excited to get students from the Core Knowledge preschool."

—*Monica Gray, Clarendon Public Schools, Clarendon, Arkansas*

"As our first school year comes to a close, we are amazed with the knowledge our students acquired in such a short period of time. The rich literacy component has made story time an exciting and meaningful part of our day. Students look forward to reading and exploring books."

—*Noeila Montaner, The Thinking Child Learning Center, Florida City, Florida, a Core Knowledge preschool*

"I am so pleased with my children's progress from using Core Knowledge preschool! They are going into kindergarten ready to read, and I know they will be successful!"

—*Bernice Richardson, preschool teacher, Baltimore, Maryland*

"We prefer the Core Knowledge preschool program simply because it works. . . . The results are apparent when our young people test for kindergarten."

—*Shay Gillespie, Head of the Class Learning Center, Monticello, Arkansas, a Core Knowledge preschool*

THE
CORE KNOWLEDGE
SERIES

Resource Books from
PRESCHOOL THROUGH GRADE SIX

DELTA TRADE PAPERBACKS

THE CORE KNOWLEDGE SERIES

What Your
PRESCHOOLER
Needs to Know

Read-Alouds
to Get Ready for
Kindergarten

E. D. HIRSCH, JR.
LINDA BEVILACQUA

WHAT YOUR PRESCHOOLER NEEDS TO KNOW
A Delta Trade Paperback / April 2008

PUBLISHED BY BANTAM DELL
A Division of Random House, Inc.
New York, New York

All rights reserved
Copyright © 2008 by Core Knowledge Foundation
Cover photograph © Photodisc/Media Bakery LLC

Book design by greenink.design

Delta is a registered trademark of Random House, Inc.,
and the colophon is a trademark of Random House, Inc.

LIBRARY OF CONGRESS CATALOGING-IN-PUBLICATION DATA

What your preschooler needs to know / [edited by]
E. D. Hirsch, Jr., Linda Bevilacqua.
p. cm.
Includes bibliographical references and index.
ISBN 978-0-385-34198-1 (trade pbk.: alk. paper)
1. Reading (Preschool) 2. Language arts (Preschool)
3. Reading—Parent participation.
I. Hirsch, E. D. (Eric Donald), 1928- II. Bevilacqua, Linda.
LB1140.5.R4W48 2008
372.21--dc22
2007027551

PRINTED IN CHINA
PUBLISHED SIMULTANEOUSLY IN CANADA

www.bantamdell.com

TOP 10 9 8 7 6 5 4 3

Par /.Teach.
J
372.59
Wha
Main

With love to my parents
and my daughters,
Alyssa and Gretchen

— L.B.

A NOTE TO PARENTS AND TEACHERS

THIS BOOK IS INTENDED to be read aloud, actively shared, and discussed with preschoolers. We have provided a brief introduction with advice for the reader, parent or teacher, at the beginning of each section and have also included suggestions and ideas in sidebars throughout the book. Additional advice for building on the foundation provided in the read-aloud selections is also included in the back of the book.

Preschoolers need many different learning experiences in order to get ready for kindergarten. Reading aloud together is just one of them. While the read-aloud selections in this book will open up new worlds and begin to lay a rich foundation of knowledge that will serve young children well as they enter school, preschoolers do best when they put their learning to action as well.

For that reason, the Core Knowledge Foundation has created two activity books to accompany this read-aloud anthology, representing two years of fun and engaging educational moments. Each book is full of games and activities, whimsically illustrated in full color and designed to build the skills that young children will need to be fully ready for the early reading, writing, and math instruction they will receive in kindergarten.

What Your Preschooler Needs to Know: Activities to Get Ready for Kindergarten, Volumes 1 and 2, were written by the same team that created this book. These activity books are available for purchase from the Core Knowledge Foundation. They may be ordered by phone at (800) 238-3233 or online at www.coreknowledge.org.

Contents

1   FOR PARENTS: Introduction
by E. D. Hirsch, Jr.

Poems

6   Singing Time *by Rose Fyleman*
6   Pussy Cat, Pussy Cat
7   Raindrops *by Aileen Fisher*
7   Doctor Foster
8   Ride a Cock Horse
8   Polly Put the Kettle On
9   At the Seaside
by Robert Louis Stevenson

Rhyming Words
10   Rain, Rain Go Away
10   Diddle Diddle Dumpling,
My Son John
11   A-Hunting We Will Go
11   Pease Porridge
12   Wee Willie Winkie
12   The Old Woman Must Stand
at the Tub
13   Hickety Pickety, My Black Hen
13   There Was a Crooked Man
14   Tom, Tom the Piper's Son
14   Higglety, Pigglety, Pop!
by Samuel Goodrich
15   Peter, Peter, Pumpkin Eater
15   The Worm *by Ralph Bergengren*
16   An Old Person of Ware
by Edward Lear
16   Once I Saw a Little Bird
17   Bat, Bat

17   To Market, To Market
18   One Misty, Moisty Morning
18   Bobby Shaftoe

Clap Along!
19   Ring Around the Rosey
19   Pat-a-Cake
20   Lucy Locket
20   One for the Money
20   Jack-o Lantern *by Aileen Fisher*
21   Who Stole the Cookie
from the Cookie Jar?

Fingerplay
22   This Little Piggy Went to Market
22   Where Is Thumbkin?
23   One Potato, Two Potato
23   Two Little Blackbirds
24   Here Is the Beehive
24   Open, Shut Them
25   The Eensy, Weensy Spider
25   Five Little Monkeys

Move Around!
26   This Is the Way the Ladies Ride
26   Teddy Bear
27   The Pancake *by Christina Rossetti*
27   Jump or Jiggle *by Evelyn Beyer*

Beginning Sounds
28   Betty Botter
29   Peter Piper
29   Jilliky Jolliky *by Jack Prelutsky*
30   Rumpitty, Tumpitty
by Jack Prelutsky
30   Tippety, Tippety

Songs

32 Hush, Little Baby
33 Kookaburra
33 Oh, Dear, What Can the Matter Be?
34 Pop Goes the Weasel
34 Did You Ever See a Lassie?
35 Are You Sleeping?
35 A Tisket, A Tasket
36 John Jacob Jingleheimer Schmidt
36 Lazy Mary
37 Five Little Ducks
38 I Know an Old Lady
39 Oh Where, Oh Where Has My Little Dog Gone?
39 You Are My Sunshine
40 The Teddy Bears' Picnic
42 Happy Birthday to You
42 Oats, Peas, Beans, and Barley Grow
43 Twinkle, Twinkle, Little Star
43 Rock-a-Bye, Baby
44 Do You Know the Muffin Man?
44 Row, Row, Row Your Boat
45 I'm a Little Teapot
45 Head and Shoulders, Knees and Toes
46 Looby Loo
46 Do Your Ears Hang Low?
47 Here We Go Round the Mulberry Bush
48 Yankee Doodle
48 If You're Happy and You Know It
49 Bingo
49 The Wheels on the Bus
50 Old MacDonald

Stories

52 Goldilocks and the Three Bears
60 The Gingerbread Man
67 The Little Red Hen
72 The Three Little Pigs
80 How Turtles Got Their Shells (Native American folktale)
85 Why Flies Buzz (African folktale)
93 The Lion and the Mouse (Aesop's fable)
97 The City Mouse and the Country Mouse (Aesop's fable)

History

104 The First Americans
110 George Washington and the Cherry Tree
114 Betsy Ross and the American Flag
117 Abraham Lincoln, Log Cabin President
121 Martin Luther King, Jr., A Man of Peace

Science

126 Animals Are Living Things
Animals have different kinds of bodies
Animals move in different ways
Animals have ways to protect themselves

Animals eat plants or other animals
Animals grow up and change
  as they grow
Some animals live and work together
Animals live in different habitats

142 Humans Are Special Animals
Humans are adaptable
Humans have amazing bodies
Humans use five senses
Humans have babies
Humans want to stay healthy

149 Plants Are Living Things
There are many different kinds of
  plants
Plants have different parts
Most plants start growing from seeds
Plants go through stages as they grow
Plants make food for people
Plants are important in our world

156 Water Is Important
Water can take different forms
Some things float, some things sink

159 Light Helps Us See
People turn on lights at night
Light passes through some things but
  not through others

162 Air Is Invisible, But It's Everywhere
Air takes up space
Moving air makes sounds
Air can push things when it moves

Art

166 Noah's Ark *by Edward Hicks*
167 The New Pets *by Emile Munier*
168 The Old Stagecoach
   by Jonathan Eastman Johnson
169 Domino Players *by Horace Pippin*
170 Sunday after the Sermon
   by Romare Bearden
171 The Snail *by Henri Matisse*
172 People and Dog in Sun *by Joan Miró*
173 Senecio *by Paul Klee*
174 The Sleeping Gypsy
   by Henri Rousseau
175 Rhythm *by Sonia Delaunay*
176 The Little Dancer *by Edgar Degas*
177 Blue Hippo

What Parents of Preschoolers Need to Know

181 Choosing a Preschool for Your Child
185 Is Your Child Ready for Kindergarten?
189 Reading Aloud with Your Child
195 Enjoying Music with
   Your Preschooler

197 Resources
197 *Great Books for Preschoolers*
201 *Great Music for Preschoolers*
203 *About the Core Knowledge Foundation*
205 *About the Authors*
207 *About the Illustrators*
209 *Credits*

Introduction

Ah, the happy years before school, the carefree time before that dreaded day when the young child becomes, as Shakespeare put it:

> *The whining school-boy, with his satchel*
> *And shining morning face, creeping like snail*
> *Unwillingly to school.*

For children who are ready for the school experience, kindergarten and first grade can be exceedingly happy and absorbing times. No creeping unwillingly for them! But that certainly isn't true of children who are not ready. Usually they will not enjoy the challenging early years of schooling. And even their futures might be compromised, since researchers have determined that children who have fallen behind in first grade tend not to catch up academically. As a consequence, the educational importance of the early years, from 2 to 5, has become increasingly well-known by psychologists and policy makers, and recently by the general public. State legislatures are beginning to offer universal preschool programs, available to all children.

WHAT PARENTS NEED TO KNOW ABOUT SCHOOL READINESS

During the past twenty-five years, however, there has been a barrier to effective preschooling, whether at home or at a school. That barrier has been a set of romantic ideas about early childhood, ideas that are widespread among some early-childhood experts and the general public. An American parent who picks up this book may have heard things like the following: that teaching pre-literacy and pre-math skills to preschoolers is unnatural, premature, and developmentally inappropriate; that such exposure distracts from healthier, more natural learning experiences; that it can be injurious to the child. These romantic ideas about early childhood have exerted a huge influence in American thought, but they are now thought by leading psychologists to be misleading and over-simplified. There is, in fact, great benefit and great fun to be gained by engaging young children in suitable educational activities.

In the United States today, some children do come to school ready to learn; generally, they are fortunate enough to come from privileged and educated families that understand the importance of these early formative years and have the capability to make the most of them. Many, many other children, though, are not ready when they enter kindergarten. While they may come from loving and well-intentioned families, often their parents have neither the financial resources nor the free time to ensure that their children engage in educationally productive experiences, either at preschool or at home. These children enter kindergarten under a severe academic disadvantage. They do not know the words and things they need to know in order to thrive in kindergarten and first grade. They do not understand things that other children understand, and they fall further behind with each passing grade.

RESEARCH ON THE IMPORTANT PRESCHOOL YEARS

The significance of this early disadvantage and its deleterious consequences cannot be overstated. One study (Hart and Risley, 1995) followed children from infancy through the elementary grades. Researchers meticulously examined everything that went on in the children's homes during the early years, then evaluated the children during their preschool years, again in kindergarten, and in third grade. Here are some highlights of their findings:

The number of words spoken to children throughout infancy and early childhood varied tremendously from family to family, and the amount of language children heard directly correlated to family income level. For example, children from the poorest families heard less language than children from working-class families. And children from both these groups heard far fewer words than children from families in which parents were professionals.

Based on these findings, researchers were able to extrapolate that, by the time children entered school, those from the professional families would have accumulated experience with nearly 45 million words, while those from the poorest families would have had experience with only 13 million words—a 30-million-word gap! Not only was there a difference in the sheer number of words that children heard, but also in the variety and the complexity of the language heard.

The number of words and the richness and complexity of the language that a child heard in his family setting, this study found, was predictive of the child's own vocabulary and early academic skills when they were evaluated in preschool and the early grades. Briefly put, children who heard more words had more words in their own vocabulary. Furthermore, the children with stronger language skills learned to read more easily and effectively than the children with weaker vocabularies.

Other studies (Jager-Adams, 1990) found that a child's reading proficiency at the end of first grade is highly predictive of:

- *Reading ability in later grades*
- *High school graduation*
- *Financial income as an adult*

Combine the two studies, and you have the picture of how important school readiness is to a child's future. Those children to whom parents read, speak, and present language describing the world of things and ideas begin school more ready to absorb all that they will be offered, and it promises to make a difference to them—and to their society—for the rest of their lives.

Despite such findings, the record shows that the children of America are not getting the most out of the public education that this nation offers. Perhaps most staggering of all, reading proficiency tests administered nationally throughout the country have recently shown that as many as 78% of the children tested fall below the proficiency level at the fourth-grade level. This figure suggests that all families, not just those in dire poverty or with little education, could be doing better at helping their children enter kindergarten ready to learn.

The good news is that we do know ways to prevent these dire consequences. Thanks to years of research, observation, and practice, we know what children need to learn and what experiences they should have before entering kindergarten. Now we just need parents and preschools to put this knowledge into practice.

WHAT IS CORE KNOWLEDGE?

Core Knowledge is an educational program designed to provide a guided, direct, and effective way of providing all children the knowledge and skills that only the favored few have possessed in the past. The program has been developed over many years and with the contributions of many experts, under the auspices of the non-profit Core Knowledge Foundation, and all proceeds from the program go back to the foundation to help more and more parents and children.

The Core Knowledge Foundation has developed educational guides from preschool through grade eight. The preschool program, on which this book is based, has been in use for over a decade among children from all social groups and in many settings across the country; it has been field-tested and refined over the years. The research evidence for its effectiveness is now overwhelming, and can be viewed at *www.coreknowledge.org*.

THE CORE KNOWLEDGE SCHOOL READINESS PROGRAM

The Core Knowledge preschool program was developed after consulting the most distinguished developmental psychologists and observing the most effective practices throughout the world. The rationale behind the selectivity and sequence of the Core Knowledge materials, now well accepted, was first developed in my 1987 book, *Cultural Literacy*. Intrinsic to the Core Knowledge Preschool Program, whether for schools or for home, is its *careful sequencing* of social and academic skills, with a strong emphasis on the knowledge that is most useful and productive for children living in American society today.

Granted, you will find plenty of other read-aloud books that are well illustrated and attractive individually. So what do the Core Knowledge preschool family materials have that others on the market do not have? Unlike other pre-kindergarten home education products, the Core Knowledge Home Preschool books are based on an overarching set of goals for learning at the preschool level, for children aged three through five. Only the Core Knowledge Home Preschool Program offers a package of readings and activities, totally coordinated to follow a cumulative sequence of essential knowledge and skills, derived from sound research. These readings and companion workbooks follow a month-by-month pattern that has been vetted by international researchers and tested over many years, with proved effectiveness. In this read-aloud book and the activity book materials accompanying it, you will find a coordinated set of simple and fun activities that family members can share with children, knowing that they are working together to get their children ready for kindergarten.

There are already more than a thousand Core Knowledge preschool classes operating across the country, following exactly this sequence of lessons and activities. The number of Core Knowledge Preschools continues to grow rapidly as their rationale and efficacy become more widely known. We at the Core Knowledge Foundation believe that all parents should also be offered this opportunity to prepare their children for a happy, productive time in school—and for the rest of their lives.

— E. D. HIRSCH, JR.

Poems

■ Poems are fun to read out loud and recite together. Their short length makes them the perfect introduction to the kinds of formal written language that your child will later encounter in stories. The rhythmic and musical combination of sounds and words invite her to play with language, experiment with rhymes, and make up nonsense words. This type of play draws attention to the sounds of spoken language, an important skill that she will need later on when she learns to read.

Reciting poems with repeating refrains helps sharpen a child's memory. Other sorts of poems offer opportunities for fingerplay, for acting out, and for building small and large motor coordination.

Alongside the various poems offered here, we note how each one contributes to your child's learning pleasure.

Singing Time
by Rose Fyleman

I wake in the morning early
And always, the very first thing,
I poke my head and I sit up in bed
And I sing and I sing and I sing.

Pussy Cat, Pussy Cat

Pussy cat, pussy cat, where have you been?
I've been to London to visit the queen.
Pussy cat, pussy cat, what did you there?
I frightened a little mouse under her chair.

Raindrops

by Aileen Fisher

How brave a ladybug must be!
Each drop of rain is as big as she.
Can you imagine what you'd do
If raindrops fell as big as you?

Doctor Foster

Doctor Foster went to Gloster
In a shower of rain.
He stepped in a puddle,
Up to his middle,
And never went there again.

Ride a Cock Horse

Ride a cock horse to Banbury Cross
To see a fine lady upon a white horse.
With rings on her fingers and bells on her toes,
She shall have music wherever she goes.

Polly Put the Kettle On

Polly put the kettle on,
Polly put the kettle on,
Polly put the kettle on,
And we'll all have tea.

Sukey take it off again,
Sukey take it off again,
Sukey take it off again,
They've all gone away.

At the Seaside
by Robert Louis Stevenson

When I was down beside the sea
A wooden spade they gave to me
To dig the sandy shore.

My holes were empty like a cup.
In every hole the sea came up,
Till it could come no more.

Rain, Rain Go Away

Rain, rain go away,
Come again another day,
Little *[your child's name]* wants to play.

Diddle Diddle Dumpling, My Son John

Diddle diddle dumpling, my son John,
Went to bed with his trousers on.
One shoe off and one shoe on,
Diddle diddle dumpling, my son John.

RHYMING WORDS

A-Hunting We Will Go

A-hunting we will go,
A-hunting we will go,
We'll catch a fox
And put him in a box
And then we'll let him go.

RHYMING WORDS

Pease Porridge

Pease Porridge hot,
Pease Porridge cold,
Pease Porridge in the pot
Nine days old.

Some like it hot,
Some like it cold,
Some like it in the pot
Nine days old.

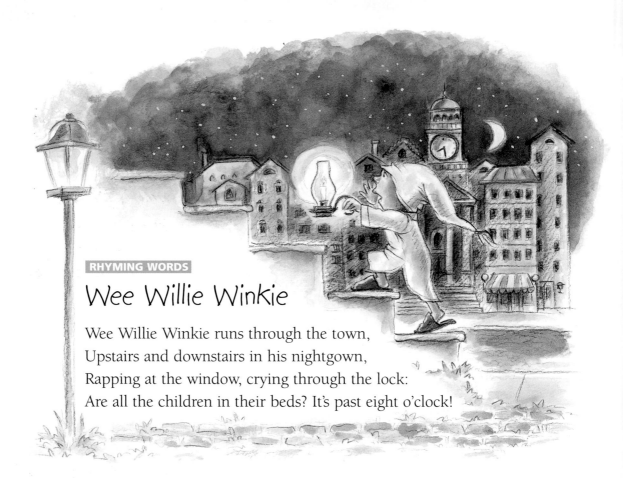

Wee Willie Winkie

Wee Willie Winkie runs through the town,
Upstairs and downstairs in his nightgown,
Rapping at the window, crying through the lock:
Are all the children in their beds? It's past eight o'clock!

The Old Woman Must Stand at the Tub

The old woman must stand
   at the tub, tub, tub,
The dirty clothes to rub, rub, rub.
But when they are clean
   and fit to be seen,
I'll dress like a lady
   and dance on the green.

RHYMING WORDS

Hickety Pickety, My Black Hen

Hickety pickety, my black hen,
She lays eggs for gentlemen.
Gentlemen come every day
To see what my black hen doth lay.

RHYMING WORDS

There Was a Crooked Man

There was a crooked man and he walked a crooked mile.
He found a crooked sixpence against a crooked stile.
He bought a crooked cat, which caught a crooked mouse,
And they all lived together in a little crooked house.

Tom, Tom the Piper's Son

Tom, Tom the piper's son
Learned to play when he was young.
And with his horn, he made such noise
He always pleased all the girls and boys.

Higglety, Pigglety, Pop!

by Samuel Goodrich

Higglety, pigglety, pop!
The dog has eaten the mop;
The pig's in a hurry,
The cat's in a flurry,
Higglety, pigglety, pop!

RHYMING WORDS

Peter, Peter, Pumpkin Eater

Peter, Peter, pumpkin eater,
Had a wife and couldn't keep her.
He put her in a pumpkin shell
And there he kept her very well.

RHYMING WORDS

The Worm by Ralph Bergengren

When the earth is turned in spring
The worms are fat as anything.
And birds come flying all around
To eat the worms right off the ground.
They like worms just as much as I
Like bread and milk and apple pie.
And once, when I was very young,
I put a worm right on my tongue.
I didn't like the taste a bit,
And so I didn't swallow it.
But oh, it makes my mother squirm
Because she thinks I ate that worm!

An Old Person of Ware

by Edward Lear

There was an old person of Ware,
Who rode on the back of a bear:
When they asked, "Does it trot?"
He said, "Certainly not!
He's a Moppsikon Floppsikon bear!"

Once I Saw a Little Bird

Once I saw a little bird
Come hop, hop, hop.
So I cried, Little bird,
Will you stop, stop, stop?
I was going to the window
To say, How do you do?
But he shook his little tail
And away he flew.

RHYMING WORDS

Bat, Bat

Bat, bat,
Come under my hat,
And I'll give you
   a slice of bacon
And when I bake
I'll give you a cake,
If I am not mistaken.

RHYMING WORDS

To Market, To Market

To market, to market,
To buy a fat pig.
Home again, home again,
Jiggety-jig.

To market, to market,
To buy a fat hog.
Home again, home again,
Jiggety-jog.

To market, to market,
To buy a plum bun.
Home again, home again,
Market is done.

One Misty, Moisty Morning

One misty moisty morning,
When cloudy was the weather,
I chanced to meet an old man
Clothed all in leather.
He began to compliment
And I began to grin,
How do you do, how do you do,
How do you do again!

Bobby Shaftoe

Bobby Shaftoe's gone to sea,
Silver buckles on his knee.
He'll come back and marry me,
Bonny Bobby Shaftoe.

Bobby Shaftoe's bright and fair,
Combing down his yellow hair.
He's my love forever more,
Bonny Bobby Shaftoe.

Bobby Shaftoe's looking out.
All his ribbons flew about.
All the ladies gave a shout,
Hey for Bobby Shaftoe!

Ring Around the Rosey

Clap for every syllable, not to the beat.

Ring around the rosey,
A pocket full of posies
Ashes, ashes,
We all fall down.

Pat-a-Cake

Clap for every syllable, not to the beat.

Pat-a-cake, pat-a-cake, baker's man!
Bake me a cake as fast as you can.
Pat it and prick it
and mark it with a *[child's initial]*,
And put it in the oven
　　for *[child's name]* and me.

Lucy Locket

Clap for every syllable,
not to the beat.

Lucy Locket lost her pocket,
Kitty Fisher found it.
Not a penny was there in it,
Only ribbon round it.

One for the Money

Clap for every syllable,
not to the beat.

One for the money,
Two for the show,
Three to make ready,
And four to go!

Jack-o-Lantern by Aileen Fisher

Clap for every syllable, not to the beat.

Jack-o-lantern, Jack-o-lantern,
orange-front-and-back-o-lantern,
sitting-on-the-sill-o-lantern,
where's you sister Jill-o-lantern?

Who Stole the Cookie from the Cookie Jar?

Begin by speaking both parts. After several repetitions, your child can join in, as if you were having a conversation.

Parent: Who stole the cookie
from the cookie jar?
[Child's name] stole the cookie
from the cookie jar!

Child: Who, me?

Parent: Yes, you.

Child: Not I.

Parent: Then who?

Child: *[Parent's—or another person's—name]*
stole the cookie from the cookie jar.

Trade parts and repeat the poem.

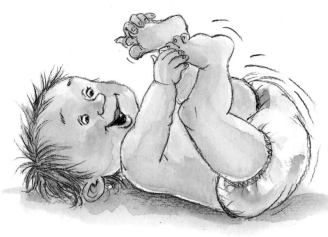

This Little Piggy Went to Market

Wiggle your child's toes, one for each line, beginning with the big one.

This little piggy went to market.
This little piggy stayed home.
This little piggy had roast beef,
And this little piggy had none.
And this little piggy cried
"Wee-wee-wee-wee," all the way home.

Where Is Thumbkin?

Present the thumb or finger named in the verse, first on one hand and then, in response, on the other. Wiggle each one during the "conversation," then hide each hand behind your back ("run away") until the next verse.

Where is thumbkin?
Where is thumbkin?
Here I am,
Here I am.
How are you today, sir?
Very well I say, sir.
Run away,
Run away.

Where is pointer? . . .
Where is middle finger? . . .
Where is ring finger? . . .
Where is pinkie? . . .

FINGERPLAY

One Potato,
Two Potato

In a circle, each child puts a fist into the middle. One among them taps each fist as the verse counts out numbers. The person whose fist is identified as "more" at the verse's end plays "It" in a game of Tag or Hide & Seek.

One potato, two potato,
Three potato, four,
Five potato, six potato,
Seven potato, more.

FINGERPLAY

Two Little Blackbirds

Make two fists, then wiggle your thumbs, one for Jack and one for Jill. Put your fist behind your back when each bird flies away, then bring it back into view when the bird comes back.

Two little blackbirds sitting on a hill.
One named Jack and one named Jill.
Fly away, Jack!
Fly away, Jill!
Come back, Jack!
Come back, Jill!

Here Is the Beehive

*Make a fist for the beehive, then extend
a finger for each number you say.*

Here is the beehive. Where are the bees?
They're hiding away so nobody sees.
Soon they'll come creeping out of their hive,
One, two, three, four, five. *Buzz-z-z-z!*

Open, Shut Them

*Model this hand dance so your child learns to do it as you recite
the poem together: For the first stanza, open your hands flat
or shut them into fists. For the second, walk your fingers up
your chest to each part of your face. For the third, end up
by covering your eyes; then peek out.*

Open, shut them, open, shut them,
Give a little clap.
Open, shut them, open, shut them,
Put them in your lap.

Creep them, creep them, creep them, creep them,
Right up to your chin.
Open wide your smiling mouth
But do not let them in.

Creep them, creep them, creep them, creep them,
Past your cheeks and chin.
Open wide your smiling eyes,
Peeking in—Boo!

Repeat first verse.

FINGERPLAY

The Eensy, Weensy Spider

Help your child follow the movements that go with this poem. Touch index finger of one hand to the thumb of the other, alternating hands, to make your hands be the spider climbing the spout. Sweep hands down, then sideways for rain. Spread hands above head for sunshine. Then start again.

The eensy, weensy spider
Climbed up the waterspout.
Down came the rain
To wash the spider out.
Out came the sunshine
And dried up all the rain.
So the eensy, weensy spider
Climbed up the spout again.

Five Little Monkeys

Five little monkeys jumping on the bed,
One fell off and bumped his head,
Mama called the doctor, and the doctor said,
"No more monkeys jumping on the bed!"

Repeat the poem, reducing the number of monkeys with each verse:

Four little monkeys jumping on the bed …
Three little monkeys jumping on the bed… *etc.*

This Is the Way the Ladies Ride

You and your child can act out this verse. Hold pretend reins and prance in place: tiptoe for ladies; gallop for gentlemen; jump for farmers; leap over the hedge; slip and fall to tumble down.

This is the way the ladies ride:
Nimble, nimble, nimble, nimble.
This is the way the gentlemen ride:
A gallop, a trot, a gallop, a trot.
This is the way the farmers ride:
Jiggety jog, jiggety jog.
And when they come to a hedge—
they jump over!
And when they come to a slippery space—
They scramble, scramble, scramble:
Tumble-down, Dick!

Teddy Bear

Ask your child to dance or move as described in each line.

Teddy bear, teddy bear, turn around.
Teddy bear, teddy bear, touch the ground.
Teddy bear, teddy bear, climb the stairs.
Teddy bear, teddy bear, say your prayers.
Teddy bear, teddy bear, turn off the light.
Teddy bear, teddy bear, say goodnight.

MOVE AROUND!

The Pancake

by Christina Rossetti

Pretend to be mixing, stirring, pouring, frying, then tossing a pancake.

Mix a pancake,
Stir a pancake,
Pop it in the pan.
Fry a pancake,
Toss the pancake—
Catch it if you can.

MOVE AROUND!

Jump or Jiggle by Evelyn Beyer

Your child can make each animal movement as the line describes it.

Frogs jump
Caterpillars hump
Worms wiggle
Bugs jiggle
Rabbits hop
Horses clop
Snakes slide
Sea gulls glide
Mice creep
Deer leap
Puppies bounce
Kittens pounce
Lions stalk
But—I walk!

Betty Botter

Betty Botter bought some butter,
But, she said, this butter's bitter.
If I put it in my batter,
It will make my batter bitter,
But a bit of better butter
Will make my batter better.
So she bought a bit of butter
Better than her bitter butter,
And she put it in her batter,
And it made her batter better.
So 'twas better Betty Botter
Bought a bit of better butter.

BEGINNING SOUNDS

Peter Piper

Peter Piper picked a peck
   of pickled peppers.
Did Peter Piper pick a peck
   of pickled peppers?
If Peter Piper picked a peck
   of pickled peppers,
Where's the peck
   of pickled peppers
   Peter Piper picked?

BEGINNING SOUNDS

Jilliky Jolliky

by Jack Prelutsky

Jilliky Jolliky Jelliky Jee,
three little cooks in a coconut tree,
one cooked a peanut and one cooked a pea,
one brewed a thimble of cinnamon tea,
then they sat down to a dinner for three,
Jilliky Jolliky Jelliky Jee.

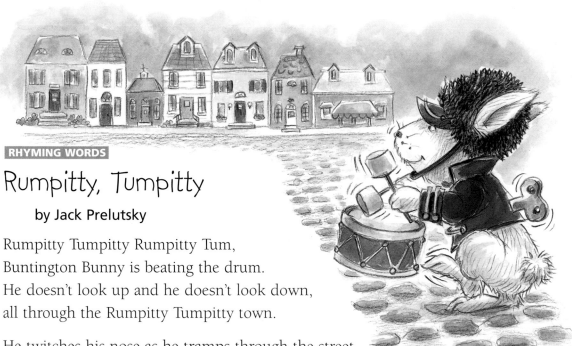

RHYMING WORDS

Rumpitty, Tumpitty

by Jack Prelutsky

Rumpitty Tumpitty Rumpitty Tum,
Buntington Bunny is beating the drum.
He doesn't look up and he doesn't look down,
all through the Rumpitty Tumpitty town.

He twitches his nose as he tramps through the street,
stamping his Rumpitty Tumpitty feet.
Rumpitty Tumpitty Rumpitty Tum,
Buntington Bunny is beating the drum.

RHYMING WORDS

Tippety, Tippety

Tippety, tippety tin,
Give me a pancake
    and I will come in.
Tippety, tippety toe,
Give me a pancake
    and I will go.

Songs

■ Young children seem to be irresistibly drawn to music. It is a form of communication, a means of creative expression, and an emotional outlet.

Listening intently to music, children are sharpening their sense of hearing and paying attention to rhythms and harmonies that are fundamentally mathematical. What's more, they enjoy music of all varieties.

Look at preschoolers' faces and bodies when they are engaged in a musical activity. They convey eagerness and enthusiasm—in a word, the sheer fun of music!

We encourage you to share a wide range of musical experiences with your child, from silly songs to classical symphonies. Lose your inhibitions (and concerns that you are not musically inclined). Sing songs together, listen to all kinds of music, have a parade, dance and enjoy!

Hush, Little Baby

Hush little baby, don't say a word.
Papa's gonna buy you a mockingbird.
If that mockingbird doesn't sing,
Papa's gonna buy you a diamond ring.
If that diamond ring turns to brass,
Papa's gonna buy you a looking glass.
If that looking glass gets broke,
Papa's gonna buy you a billy goat.
If that billy goat won't pull,
Papa's gonna buy you a cart and bull.
If that cart and bull turn over,
Papa's gonna buy you a dog named Rover.
If that dog named Rover won't bark,
Papa's gonna buy you a horse and cart.
If that horse and cart fall down,
You'll still be the sweetest little baby in town.

Kookaburra

Kookaburra sits in the old gum tree,
Merry, merry king of the bush is he.
Laugh, Kookaburra, laugh, Kookaburra,
Gay your life must be.

Oh, Dear, What Can the Matter Be?

Oh, dear, what can the matter be?
Oh, dear, what can the matter be?
Oh, dear, what can the matter be?
Johnny's so long at the fair.
He promised to buy me a basket of posies,
A garland of lilies, a garland of roses,
A little straw hat to set off the blue ribbons
That tie up my bonny brown hair.

Pop Goes the Weasel

All around the cobbler's bench,
The monkey chased the weasel.
The monkey thought 'twas all in fun.
Pop! goes the weasel.
A penny for a spool of thread,
A penny for a needle.
That's the way the money goes.
Pop! goes the weasel!

Did You Ever
See a Lassie?

Did you ever see a lassie,
   a lassie, a lassie,
Did you ever see a lassie
   go this way and that?
Go this way and that way,
   and this way and that way.
Did you ever see a lassie
   go this way and that?

ROUND

Are You Sleeping?

Are you sleeping, are you sleeping,
Brother John, Brother John?
Morning bells are ringing,
morning bells are ringing!
Ding, Ding, Dong! Ding, Ding, Dong!

A Tisket, A Tasket

A tisket, a tasket,
A green and yellow basket.
I wrote a letter to my love,
And on the way I dropped it.
I dropped it, I dropped it,
On the way I dropped it.
I wrote a letter to my love,
And on the way I dropped it.

John Jacob Jingleheimer Schmidt

John Jacob Jingleheimer Schmidt,
His name is my name, too.
Whenever we go out,
The people always shout,
"There goes John Jacob Jingleheimer Schmidt!"
Dah, dah, dah, dah, dah, dah, dah.

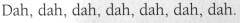

Lazy Mary

Lazy Mary, will you get up,
Will you get up, will you get up?
Lazy Mary, will you get up,
So early in the morning?

No, no, Mother, I won't get up,
I won't get up, I won't get up.
No, no, Mother, I won't get up,
So early in the morning!

MAKE NOISES

Five Little Ducks

Five little ducks that I once knew
Fat ones, skinny ones, tall ones, too.
But the one little duck with the feather on his back,
He ruled the others with a quack, quack, quack!
Quack, quack, quack! Quack, quack, quack!
He ruled the others with a quack, quack, quack!

Down to the river they would go,
Wibble, wobble, wibble, wobble, all in a row.
But the one little duck with the feather on his back,
He ruled the others with a quack, quack, quack!
Quack, quack, quack! Quack, quack, quack!
He ruled the others with a quack, quack, quack!

I Know an Old Lady

I know an old lady who swallowed a fly.
I don't know why she swallowed a fly.
Perhaps she'll die.

I know an old lady who swallowed a spider.
It wiggled and wriggled and jiggled inside her.
She swallowed the spider to catch the fly.
I don't know why she swallowed a fly. Perhaps she'll die.

I know an old lady who swallowed a bird.
How absurd to swallow a bird!
She swallowed the bird to catch the spider,
That wiggled and . . . *(repeat lines from above, 2nd line on)*

I know an old lady who swallowed a cat.
Well fancy that, she swallowed a cat!
She swallowed the cat to catch the bird . . . *(repeat)*

I know an old lady who swallowed a dog.
What a hog, to swallow a dog!
She swallowed the dog to catch the cat . . . *(repeat)*

I know an old lady who swallowed a cow.
I don't know how she swallowed a cow!
She swallowed a cow to catch the dog . . . *(repeat)*

I know an old lady who swallowed a horse.
She's dead, of course!

Oh Where, Oh Where Has My Little Dog Gone?

Oh where, oh where has my little dog gone?
Oh where, oh where can he be?
With his ears cut short and his tail cut long,
Oh where, oh where can he be?

You Are My Sunshine

You are my sunshine,
My only sunshine.
You make me happy
  when skies are gray.
You'll never know, dear,
How much I love you.
Please don't take
  my sunshine away.

The Teddy Bears' Picnic

If you go down to the woods today,
You're sure of a big surprise.
If you go down to the woods today,
You'd better go in disguise.
For every bear that there ever was
Will gather there for certain, because
Today's the day the teddy bears have their picnic.

Every teddy bear who's been good
Is sure of a treat today.
There's lots of marvelous things to eat
And wonderful games to play.
Beneath the trees where nobody sees,

They'll hide and seek as long as they please,
'Cause that's the way the teddy bears have their picnic.

If you go down to the woods today,
You'd better not go alone.
It's lovely down in the woods today,
But safer to stay at home.
For every bear that there ever was
Will gather there for certain, because
Today's the day the teddy bears have their picnic.

Picnic time for teddy bears,
The little teddy bears are having a lovely time today.
Watch them, catch them unawares
And see them picnic on their holiday.
See them gaily gad about.
They love to play and shout.
They never have any cares.
At six o'clock their Mommies and Daddies
Will take them home to bed,
Because they're tired little teddy bears.

Happy Birthday to You

Happy birthday to you,
Happy birthday to you,
Happy birthday, dear *[name]*,
Happy birthday to you!

Oats, Peas, Beans, and Barley Grow

Oats, peas, beans, and barley grow,
Oats, peas, beans, and barley grow,
Do you or I or anyone know,
How oats, peas, beans, and barley grow?

First the farmer sows his seeds,
Then he stands and takes his ease,
Stamps his feet, and claps his hand,
And turns around to view the land.

RHYMING WORDS

Twinkle, Twinkle, Little Star

Twinkle, twinkle little star,
How I wonder what you are.
Up above the world so high,
Like a diamond in the sky.
Twinkle, twinkle little star,
How I wonder what you are!

MOVE AROUND

Rock-a-Bye, Baby

Rock-a-bye, baby,
On the treetop.
When the wind blows,
The cradle will rock.
When the bough breaks,
The cradle will fall,
And down will come baby,
Cradle and all.

Do You Know the Muffin Man?

Do you know the muffin man,
The muffin man, the muffin man?
Do you know the muffin man
Who lives on Drury Lane?

Yes, I know the muffin man,
The muffin man, the muffin man.
Yes, I know the muffin man
Who lives on Drury Lane.

`ROUND`

Row, Row, Row Your Boat

Row, row, row your boat,
Gently down the stream.
Merrily, merrily, merrily, merrily,
Life is but a dream.

MOVE AROUND

I'm a Little Teapot

As the words say so, show your child how to put one arm out like a handle, the other out like a spout. Change sides for the second verse.

I'm a little teapot, short and stout.
This is my handle. This is my spout.
When I get all steamed up, then I shout,
"Just tip me over and pour me out!"

I'm a clever little pot, it is true.
Here's an example of what I can do.
I can change my handle with my spout
Just tip me over and pour me out.

MOVE AROUND

Head and Shoulders, Knees and Toes

Touch each body part as you sing about it.

Head and shoulders,
knees and toes,
knees and toes.
Head and shoulders,
knees and toes,
knees and toes.
Eyes and ears and mouth and nose.
Head and shoulders,
knees and toes,
knees and toes!

MOVE AROUND

Looby Loo

Sing this song in a circle. Each person places right hand into the center, then out again; left hand into the center, then out again, etc.

Here we go Looby Loo,
Here we go Looby Light,
Here we go Looby Loo,
All on a Saturday night!

You put your right hand in,
You put your right hand out,
You give your hand
   a shake, shake, shake,
And turn yourself about.

You put your left hand in, …
You put your right foot in, …

Continue with more verses, putting other body parts in—left foot, head, etc.—and finally putting whole self in.

MOVE AROUND

Do Your Ears Hang Low?

For each line, make hand movements to match the imaginary ear movements.

Do your ears hang low?
Do they wobble to and fro?
Can you tie them in a knot?
Can you tie them in a bow?
Can you throw them
   over your shoulder
Like a continental soldier?
Do your ears hang low?

MOVE AROUND

Here We Go Round the Mulberry Bush

For each verse, make movements to represent the day's activity.

Here we go round the mulberry bush,
The mulberry bush, the mulberry bush.
Here we go round the mulberry bush,
So early in the morning.

This is the way we wash our clothes,
wash our clothes, wash our clothes.
This is the way we wash our clothes,
So early Monday morning

Verses:
This is the way we
■ *iron our clothes (Tuesday)*
■ *mend our clothes (Wednesday)*
■ *scrub the floor (Thursday)*
■ *sweep the house (Friday)*
■ *bake the bread (Saturday)*
■ *go to church (Sunday)*

Yankee Doodle

During the American Revolution, a "macaroni" was someone who was all dressed up.

Yankee Doodle went to town
Riding on a pony,
Stuck a feather in his cap
And called it "macaroni."

Yankee doodle, keep it up,
Yankee doodle dandy;
Mind the music and the step,
And with the girls be handy.

MOVE AROUND

If You're Happy And You Know It

If you're happy and you know it,
Clap your hands [*clap, clap*].
If you're happy and you know it,
Clap your hands [*clap, clap*].
If you're happy and you know it,
Then your face will surely show it.
If you're happy and you know it,
Clap your hands [*clap, clap*].

Sing more verses with different actions, like "stamp your feet," "wiggle your nose," "tap your head," and "shout hooray."

Bingo

Repeat this song over and over, each time replacing a new letter in Bingo's name with a clap, until you are clapping five times without saying any letters.

There was a farmer
  who had a dog,
and Bingo was his name-o.
B-I-N-G-O,
B-I-N-G-O,
B-I-N-G-O,
And Bingo was his name-o.

MOVE AROUND

The Wheels on the Bus

For each verse, make hand movements to match: wheels spinning, wipers swishing, people going up and down, driver pointing back, baby crying.

The wheels on the bus go round and round,
round and round, round and round.
The wheels on the bus go round and round
All through the town.

Verses:
- *The wipers on the bus go swish, swish, swish*
- *The people on the bus go up and down*
- *The driver on the bus goes "Move on back..."*
- *The baby on the bus goes "Wah, wah, wah..."*

Old MacDonald

Old MacDonald had a farm, E-I-E-I-O.
And on this farm he had some chicks, E-I-E-I-O.
With a chick-chick here, and a chick-chick there,
Here a chick, there a chick, everywhere a chick-chick.
Old MacDonald had a farm, E-I-E-I-O.

Old MacDonald had a farm, E-I-E-I-O.
And on this farm he had some ducks, E-I-E-I-O.
With a quack-quack here, and a quack-quack there,
Here a quack, there a quack, everywhere a quack-quack.
Old MacDonald had a farm, E-I-E-I-O.

*Continue with more verses about different animals and sounds:
cow: mow-moo, sheep: baa-baa, pig: oink-oink, horse: neigh-neigh,
dog: bow-wow, cat: meow-meow.*

Stories

WHAT IS THE ONE THING that you can do to make a difference in your child's early development to ensure later success in school?

The answer, without question: Read aloud every day with your child. In many households, story time is the one time when parents and children retreat from the barrage of everyday demands to cuddle and share a pleasant experience together. Beyond that, reading stories aloud offers a multitude of learning possibilities.

Parents can enrich the learning process by making every story come alive, inviting children to think and talk about plot, characters, and conflict. Think of story time not as a one-sided read-aloud event but as a dynamic dialogue between you and your child. (For more on these ideas, see "Reading Aloud to Your Child" elsewhere in this book.)

Here we offer a number of traditional fairy tales and fables, annotated with ideas on when a parent might stop and talk about words or ideas important to the story.

Goldilocks and the Three Bears

Take a Look

Point to each bear as he or she is introduced. Talk about their three sizes. "What else can you see in this picture that comes in the same three sizes?"

ONCE UPON A TIME, a long time ago, there were three bears who lived together in a cozy cottage in the woods. There was a great big Papa Bear. There was a middle-sized Mama Bear. And there was a teeny tiny Baby Bear.

One morning Papa Bear cooked some porridge for breakfast. When it was ready, Papa Bear poured his own porridge into a great big bowl. Next he poured Mama Bear's porridge into a middle-sized bowl. And then Papa Bear poured Baby Bear's porridge into a teeny tiny bowl. He placed each bowl on the kitchen table. The three bears were all very hungry, but they could tell that the porridge was much too hot to eat.

They opened the windows and opened the door so that the chilly morning air would cool the porridge. They decided that while they were waiting, they would go for a walk in the woods. Out they went, leaving the porridge behind on the table.

Now this very same morning, a young girl with golden yellow hair named Goldilocks had also gone out for a walk. She lived in another part of these same woods. But being a little girl out all by herself, poor Goldilocks had become lost in the forest.

She wandered about, seeing nothing but trees, trees, trees, and more trees. Tired and worn out, she finally came to the little cottage in the woods that belonged to the three bears.

New Words
Does your child understand the word "porridge"? It's hot cereal. Help her think of some examples of porridge that she might eat, like oatmeal, cream of wheat, or grits.

Goldilocks noticed right away that the doors and windows of the house were wide open. She smelled a delicious aroma coming from the house, and that aroma seemed to be inviting her inside. She tiptoed up to the open door and peeked in. No one was there, but she did see the three bowls of porridge on the table.

Now you might think that Goldilocks would turn around and walk away, since this was not her house. But not Goldilocks! She walked right in.

What About You?

Take a moment to ask your child what he would do if he came upon a house in the woods with the door wide open. "Would you walk right in?" Talk with him about his answer.

Goldilocks went straight to the table with the three bowls of porridge. She was quite hungry after having been lost in the forest, and she decided to have a little something to eat. First she used the great big spoon to taste the porridge in the great big bowl. But it was too hot. "Yikes!" said Goldilocks. The porridge burned her tongue.

Next, Goldilocks used the middle-sized spoon to taste the porridge in the middle-sized bowl. "Yuck!" said Goldilocks. That porridge was too cold.

Then, using the teeny tiny spoon, she tasted the porridge in the teeny tiny bowl. "Yum!" said Goldilocks. It was just right. She gobbled up every last drop of porridge from the teeny tiny bowl.

Now Goldilocks looked all around the room. She saw three chairs—a great big chair, a middle-sized chair, and a teeny tiny chair. "I think I'll take a little rest before I continue on my way," said Goldilocks.

So she sat down in the great big chair. But it was too hard. "Ouch!" cried Goldilocks as she wiggled out of the great big chair. Next Goldilocks sat down in the middle-sized chair. But it was too soft. "Oof!" said Goldilocks as she climbed out of the middle-sized chair. Then she sat down in the teeny tiny chair. "Aah!" said Goldilocks. And just as she was thinking that the teeny tiny chair was just right, *crick, crack, crash!*—the chair broke into pieces and Goldilocks fell to the floor!

What About You?
Ask your child, "How do you think Goldilocks must have felt when the teeny tiny chair broke into pieces under her and she fell on the floor?"

Startled, Goldilocks stood up. She was still tired, so she looked for another place to rest. She went upstairs and found three beds. There was a great big bed, a middle-sized bed, and a teeny tiny bed.

First Goldilocks tried to lie down on the great big bed, but it was too high. Next she laid down on the middle-sized bed, but it was too low. Finally she laid down on the teeny tiny bed. It was just right. The teeny tiny bed was so comfortable, Goldilocks fell fast asleep.

Take a Look

Before reading what the bears said, look at the picture opposite and ask your child what the bears might have seen that gave them the idea that someone had been inside their house.

Just as Goldilocks was falling asleep upstairs, the three bears were coming back from their walk. They opened the door and came inside. Hungrier than ever, they went to the table to eat their porridge. They knew right away that someone had been inside their house, because the table was not as they had left it.

Papa Bear looked at his great big bowl and cried out in a great big voice, "Someone has been eating my porridge!" Mama Bear looked at her middle-sized bowl and said in her middle-sized voice, "Someone has been eating my porridge!" Then Baby Bear looked at his teeny tiny bowl and squeaked in his teeny tiny voice, "Someone has been eating my porridge—*and has eaten it all up!*"

Then the three bears looked around. Papa Bear looked at his great big chair and cried out in his great big voice, "Someone has been sitting in my chair!" Mama Bear looked at her middle-sized chair and said in her middle-sized voice, "Someone has been sitting in my chair!" Then Baby Bear looked at the broken pieces of his teeny tiny chair and he squeaked in his teeny tiny voice, "Someone has been sitting in my chair—*and has broken it all to pieces!*"

All Together

Encourage your child to repeat what the bears say, using a different voice for each bear.

Talk & Think

Talk with your child about how the bears feel in this picture. Who looks mad? Who looks sad? Why are they mad and sad?

The three bears ran upstairs to the bedroom. Papa Bear looked at his great big bed and said in his great big voice, "Someone has been sleeping in my bed!" Mama Bear looked at her middle-sized bed and said in her middle-sized voice, "Someone has been sleeping in my bed!" Then Baby Bear looked at his teeny tiny bed and squeaked in his teeny tiny voice, "Someone has been sleeping in my bed—*and here she is!*"

At this moment, the three bears' talking awakened Goldilocks. She sat straight up in that teeny tiny bed. She saw the three bears standing above her, and she cried out, "Oh my!"

She scrambled out of that teeny tiny bed as fast as she could. She leapt down the stairs and ran out the front door.

She ran and she ran and she ran and she ran, until she could not see that cottage any-more. And to this day, the three bears have never seen Goldilocks again.

How About You?
After finishing the story, ask your child why Goldilocks ran away from the bears. Does she remember a time when she ran away from something? Ask her to tell you that story.

The End

The Gingerbread Man

Talk & Think

Ask your child what kind of chores the old man might do outdoors on the farm.

Do It Yourself

Has your child ever tasted gingerbread? It would be fun to make or buy gingerbread cookies to enjoy together after you read this story.

ONCE UPON A TIME, a little old man and a little old woman lived together on a little old farm. Every day, from sunrise to sunset, the little old man worked outdoors, taking care of all the animals and all the chores on the farm. And every day, from sunrise to sunset, the little old woman worked indoors, cooking and baking the most delicious treats to eat.

One day, she decided to try something new. In a big bowl, she mixed some flour and some butter and some eggs, together with a sprinkle of cinnamon and a spoonful of ginger. She stirred and stirred until she had a ball of spicy gingerbread dough.

Now instead of just making a simple gingerbread cake, the little old woman decided to prepare a special surprise for the little old man. She rolled the dough out flat, cut it in the shape of a little man, and placed that little man on a cookie sheet. She stuck candies into the dough to make his eyes, nose, and mouth, and she added three more candies, all in a row, for his buttons. What a splendid gingerbread man he was!

The little old woman popped the cookie sheet into the hot oven and waited for the gingerbread man to bake. It wasn't long before she could smell the delicious aroma of gingerbread coming from the oven. She opened the oven door ever so slightly to see if the gingerbread man was done.

Much to her surprise, the gingerbread man sat up! Then he stood up, squeezed out the open oven door, jumped down to the kitchen floor, and ran out the front door of the house! Then he ran and he ran and he ran—down the driveway, past the sunflower garden, and past the watermelon patch.

The little old man and the little old woman ran, too, chasing after the gingerbread man. "Stop! Stop!" they shouted.

Talk & Think

Ask your child to tell you why the old woman was surprised. What did the gingerbread man do that surprised her?

Take a Look

As you read aloud, point to things as you say them: the house, the sunflower garden, the watermelon patch, for example.

But the gingerbread man ran even faster, laughing and yelling as he ran, "Run, run, as fast as you can. You can't catch me. I'm the gingerbread man!" Try as they might, no matter how fast they ran, the little old man and the little old woman could not catch the gingerbread man. Soon he was out of sight.

The gingerbread man ran and ran down the road, past a cow grazing in the field. "Stop! Stop!" yelled the cow. "Gingerbread men make good snacks!"

But the gingerbread man just laughed and said, "Run, run, as fast as you can. You can't catch me. I'm the gingerbread man! I ran from the little old man. I ran from the little old woman. And now I'll run away from you!" Try as she might, no matter how fast she ran, the cow could not catch the gingerbread man. He crossed the railroad tracks on the way out of town, and soon he was out of sight.

And still the gingerbread man ran and ran. He came to a yard where a sleepy cat lay dozing in the sun. A gentle breeze was blowing and, as the gingerbread man came running by, the spicy scent of gingerbread tickled the cat's nose. Smacking his lips, the cat jumped up and cried, "Stop! Stop! You smell so delicious. Stop and let me have a bite to eat."

All Together

This story has many recurring phrases, like "Run, run, as fast as you can." Encourage your child to say them with you as you read the story together.

Talk & Think

As you read this part of the story, ask your child to tell you why the cow and the cat want to catch the gingerbread man.

But the gingerbread man just laughed and said, "Run, run, as fast as you can. You can't catch me. I'm the gingerbread man! I ran from the cow. I ran from the little old man and the little old woman. And now I'll run away from you!" And try as he might, no matter how fast he ran, the cat could not catch the gingerbread man, who was soon out of sight.

Still the gingerbread man ran and ran, past the trees and through the forest. Soon he came upon a red fox, sitting on the bank of a river.

Now the gingerbread man was feeling rather smug and sure of himself. After all, he had run faster than everyone! So before the fox had even said a word, the gingerbread man teased him and said, "Run, run, as fast as you can. You can't catch me. I'm the gingerbread man! I ran from the cat. I ran from the cow. I ran from the little old man and the little old woman. And now I'll run away from you!"

Talk & Think
Ask your child how the gingerbread man feels after running away from the woman, the man, the cat, and the cow. Give her time to answer. Then you can suggest words like "proud," "fast," and even "smug."

Now the red fox was a rather clever fellow, as foxes usually are. He replied in a nonchalant voice, "Why in the world would I want to run after you?"

That made the gingerbread man stop and think. He said, "Why? Because I would be very tasty to eat. That's why everyone else has been trying to catch me!"

"Well," said the fox. "That explains it. But you see, I've just had my lunch. I couldn't eat another bite even if I wanted to."

The gingerbread man stood and thought a while about what the fox had said. He was still thinking when the fox asked, "By the way, where are you going now?"

"That way," said the gingerbread man, pointing across the river.

"Well, perhaps I can help you," said the fox. "You will get all wet if you try to cross the river by yourself. I'd be happy to give you a ride to the other side. You can sit on the tip of my tail while I swim across."

"Why, thank you," said the gingerbread man, and he hopped on the tip of the fox's tail.

After swimming part of the way across the river, the fox called out, "The water is getting deeper, my friend. Perhaps you would be more comfortable riding on my head."

"That's thoughtful of you," said the gingerbread man, and he slid down the fox's tail and climbed onto his head.

New Words
Tell your child that when someone speaks "in a nonchalant voice" it means he sounds as if he doesn't care or wasn't thinking much about it. Try together to say what the fox said in a nonchalant voice.

What About You?
Ask your child if he thinks it's a good idea for the gingerbread man to ride across the river with the fox. Talk about his answer.

The fox kept paddling across the river. As he approached the bank on the other side, he called out to the gingerbread man, seeming to be so friendly, "How are you doing? The water is getting even deeper. Perhaps you would be more comfortable if you were to ride on the tip of my nose for the rest of the journey."

"Why, yes," said the gingerbread man. "That's a good idea." And he perched himself on the end of the fox's nose.

"Thank y—," the gingerbread man started to say. But before he could even finish, the sly fox gave a little twist of his head, tossed the gingerbread man ever so lightly into the air, and opened his mouth wide. *Chomp! Smack!*

"Mmmmm," said the fox with a satisfied grin. "You are right, my friend. Gingerbread is very good to eat!"

The End

Talk & Think

Talk with your child about what happens at the end. Was the fox as friendly and helpful as he seemed? Did the gingerbread man make a mistake? What was it?

The Little Red Hen

A LITTLE RED HEN worked hard every day, but the other animals on the farm never helped.

As she was scratching around in the barnyard one day, the little red hen found some grains of wheat. "We can plant these seeds and they will grow," thought the hen. So she asked, "Who will help me plant these grains of wheat?"

"Not I," quacked the duck.

"Not I," meowed the cat.

"Not I," oinked the pig.

Take a Look

As you begin to read this story, talk about the picture with your child. What animals does he see here? Can she name every one? What sound does each of these animals make?

Do It Yourself

Maybe you and your child have planted seeds and watched them grow, just like the Little Red Hen. Talk together about what you had to do to help the seed sprout and grow.

New Words

"Grain" is a word used for some kinds of seeds. We make bread from flour, and flour is made from grain, or seeds of wheat, that have been ground up.

"Then I will do it myself," clucked the little red hen. And that is just what she did—all by herself!

Every day she checked to see how the wheat plants were growing. She pulled the weeds around them to give the wheat room to grow. By the end of the summer, those seeds of wheat had sprouted and grown into tall stalks of ripe golden grain.

When the stalks of wheat were ripe and the wheat grain was ready to be harvested from the field, the little red hen asked, "Who will help me cut the wheat?"

"Not I," quacked the duck.

"Not I," meowed the cat.

"Not I," oinked the pig.

"Then I will do it myself," clucked the little red hen. And that is just what she did—all by herself!

When she had cut the wheat, the little red hen asked, "Who will help me grind this wheat grain into flour?"

"Not I," quacked the duck.

"Not I," meowed the cat.

"Not I," oinked the pig.

"Then I will do it myself," clucked the little red hen. And that is just what she did—all by herself!

When the wheat grain had been ground into flour, the little red hen asked, "Now who will help me make this flour into bread dough?"

"Not I," quacked the duck.

"Not I," meowed the cat.

"Not I," oinked the pig.

All Together

As you read, encourage your child to repeat the recurring refrains of the story: "Not I," as each of the three animals say it, and "Then I will do it myself," along with the Little Red Hen.

"Then I will do it myself," clucked the little red hen. And that is just what she did—all by herself!

When she had mixed the dough, the little red hen asked, "Who will help me bake the bread?"

"Not I," quacked the duck.

"Not I," meowed the cat.

"Not I," oinked the pig.

"Then I will do it myself," clucked the little red hen. And that is just what she did—all by herself!

And so, all by herself, the little red hen baked a fine loaf of bread. "Now," she said, "who will help me eat the bread?"

"I will," quacked the duck

"I will," meowed the cat.

"I will," oinked the pig.

"Aha!" clucked the little red hen. "No, you will not! I planted the wheat all by myself. I cut the wheat all by myself. I ground the wheat grain into flour all by myself. I mixed the dough and baked it all by myself. And now I will eat the bread—all by myself!"

And that is what she did.

The End

THE LITTLE RED HEN

The Three Little Pigs

Take a Look

Look at the picture together. Each pig feels differently about leaving his mother. Talk with your child about how each pig feels.

ONCE UPON A TIME, there were three little pigs who lived with their mother. One day the mother pig said to the three little pigs, "You are all grown up now. It's time for you to go out into the world and live on your own."

So the three little pigs gave their mother a big hug and kiss and set out to find their own places to live.

They walked down the road, and soon the three pigs saw a man with a horse pulling a wagon full of straw.

"Why, I could build a house of straw in no time," thought the first little pig. So the first little pig said to the man, "Please, sir, may I have some straw so that I may build a house?" The kind man gave him the straw, and the first little pig built his house. He finished the house of straw very quickly—so quickly that he laid down contentedly in the shade to take a nap for the rest of the day.

The other two pigs continued on their way.

It wasn't long before they passed a man pushing a cart full of sticks. "Hmm, I could build a house of sticks," thought the second

New Words

Does your child know what straw is? It can be explained as long, dry pieces of grass. Point out the pile of straw in the picture to help explain.

little pig. "It will take a little more time than my brother's house of straw, but it will be a fine house indeed." So the second little pig said to the man, "Please, sir, may I have some sticks so that I may build a house?" The kind man gave him the sticks, and the second little pig started to build his house. He finished building his house of sticks in a little while. Then he, too, laid down contentedly in the shade near his house and began to take a nap.

The third little pig continued on his way.

In a little while, he passed a man with a wheelbarrow full of bricks. "Aha! I could build a house of bricks," thought the third little pig. "It's true that it will take more work to build a house of bricks than it took for my brothers to build their houses of straw and sticks, but it will be well worth it."

Do It Yourself

Find real examples of straw, sticks, and bricks to use as you and your child read this story. Concrete examples can help him remember and understand.

So he said to the man, "Please, sir, may I have some bricks so that I may build a house?" The kind man gave him the bricks, and the third little pig set about building his house. He worked and worked in the hot afternoon sun, taking care to lay each brick just so.

At about the same time, a mean and wretched big bad wolf came trotting down the lane. The wolf saw the first little pig napping in the shade of his straw house. "Yum, yum, that pig would make a tasty bite to eat," thought the big bad wolf.

Talk & Think

Once you have read about each of the three houses—but before you have finished the story—ask your child which house he thinks will be the strongest.

But the little pig saw him coming. The pig ran inside his house of straw, slamming the door behind him. He breathed a sigh of relief, because he remembered that his mother had told him and his brothers many times that wolves were not to be trusted.

Now the big bad wolf came right up to the house of straw. He knocked at the door and said, "Little pig, little pig, let me come in."

The little pig answered, "Not by the hair of my chinny-chin-chin."

"Then I'll huff and I'll puff and I'll blow your house down," said the wolf. And he huffed, and he puffed, and he blew the house down. As the straw blew everywhere, the first little pig ran away.

Rubbing his stomach and now feeling even hungrier, the big, bad wolf strode further down the lane. Soon he came upon the second little pig, who was napping in the shade of his house of sticks. The little pig saw him coming and ran inside.

The big bad wolf came right up to the house of sticks. He knocked on the door and said, "Little pig, little pig, let me come in."

All Together

Your child will enjoy filling in the repeating phrases in stories like this one. Once she knows the story, pause and let her say the words.

"Not by the hair of my chinny-chin-chin," answered the little pig.

"Then I'll huff and I'll puff and I'll blow your house down," said the big bad wolf. And he huffed and he puffed, and he blew down the house of sticks. The little pig ran away just in the nick of time.

Now the wolf's stomach growled loudly. He was feeling so hungry! He continued down the lane.

Soon he saw the third little pig, who had just finished his house of bricks. The little pig looked up. There were his two brother pigs, running toward him, and right behind them was the big bad wolf! All three pigs hurried into the house of bricks and locked the door behind them.

Take a Look

Talk about the picture below together. "What is happening here? What happened just before? What might happen after? What do you see far away in the picture? Whose house do you think that is?"

The big bad wolf came right up to the house of bricks. He knocked on the door, and once again he said, "Little pig, little pig, let me come in."

"Not by the hair of my chinny-chin-chin," answered the little pig.

"Then I'll huff and I'll puff and I'll blow your house down," said the big bad wolf. Well, the wolf huffed and puffed, and he puffed and he huffed, and he huffed and he puffed even more. But he could not blow down that house of bricks.

"My house is too strong for you to blow down," shouted the third little pig.

"Ha!" said the wolf. But he had a plan. "I'm stronger and smarter than any little pig," he said to himself. "I'll climb up onto the roof and get into the house through the chimney."

Now the third little pig had already guessed what the wolf might try to do, so he already had a fire blazing in the fireplace and a big kettle of water heating over the fire.

Thinking of himself as very clever, the wolf jumped down the chimney and splash! he fell right into that boiling hot water. That was the end of the big bad wolf. And the three little pigs lived happily ever after.

The End

Talk & Think
Be sure to help your child understand how a chimney connects to a fireplace.

Talk & Think
Ask your child what the three little pigs learned in this story. "What did the first two pigs do wrong? What did the third little pig do right?"

How Turtles
Got Their Shells

Take a Look

Talk together about how, in many places (maybe where you live), the leaves change colors with the seasons. Talk about the leaves in the picture above. "What color are they? And so what season must it be?"

IT WAS THE TIME of the year when the yellow leaves start falling from the aspen trees. Turtle was walking about on the ground. Up above him, he saw many birds gathering together in the trees. They were making such a lot of noise, and Turtle was curious to know what was happening.

"Don't you know?" the birds said. "We're getting ready to fly to the south for the winter."

"Why are you going to do that?" asked Turtle.

"Don't you know anything?" answered the birds. "Soon it's going to be very cold here, and the snow will begin to fall. There won't be much food to eat. Down south it will be warm, though. Summer lives there all of the time, and there's plenty of food."

As soon as the birds mentioned food, Turtle became more interested. "Can I come with you?" he asked.

"You have to be able to fly to go south with us," said the birds. "But you are a turtle, and you can't fly."

Turtle would not give up. "Isn't there some way you could take me along?" he asked. He begged and he pleaded. Finally, just to get him to stop bothering them, the birds agreed.

"Look here," they said, "can you use your mouth to hold on tightly to a stick?"

"That's no problem at all," Turtle said. "Once I grab onto something with my mouth, no one can make me let go until I am ready."

"Good," said the birds. "Then you hold on tightly to this stick. Two of us will grab the ends with our feet. That way we can lift you up and carry you with us on our way south. But remember— keep your mouth shut!"

"That's easy," said Turtle. "Now let's go south where Summer keeps all that food." Turtle grabbed on to the middle of the stick, and two big birds came and grabbed each end. They flapped their wings hard and lifted Turtle off the ground. Soon Turtle and the birds were high in the sky, heading south.

> **Talk & Think**
>
> Talk with your child about migration: the natural process of animals traveling far distances for different seasons of the year. Depending on where you live, you may be able to see birds flying south for the winter.

Turtle had never been so high off the ground before. He liked it. He could look down and see how small everything looked.

But before he and the birds had gone very far, he began to wonder where they were. He wondered about the lake down below him and the hills beyond. He wondered how far they had come and how far they would have to go to get to the south, where Summer lived. He wanted to ask the two birds all these questions—but he couldn't talk with his mouth tightly closed.

Turtle tried rolling his eyes, but the two birds just kept on flying. Then Turtle tried waving his legs at them, but they acted as if they didn't even notice. Now Turtle was getting upset. If they were going to take him south, the least they could do was tell him where they were now! "Mmmph," said Turtle, trying to get their attention. It didn't work.

Finally Turtle lost his temper.

"Why don't you listen to—" was all he said, for as soon as he opened his mouth to speak, he let go of the stick and started to fall.

Down and down and down he fell, a long, long way. Turtle was so frightened that he pulled his legs and his head into his shell for protection. He hit the ground hard, which made him ache all over. He ached so much, he didn't even notice how his shell had cracked all over when he landed so hard on the ground.

Talk & Think

Why do the trees look small to Turtle? Your child is just learning about perspective. To help, ask him to look outside, hold up his thumb, and compare it with something he sees far away.

What About You?

Ask your child how would it feel to be so high up, holding on to a stick in your mouth? "What would you want to say? If you said it, what would happen?"

Talk & Think

This story is a fable—a make-believe story that tries to explain something in nature. This story never happened, but it is true that turtle shells look cracked. It is also true that some turtles spend the winter underwater. Look in library books for more to read about turtles and hibernation.

Turtle was very unhappy. He wanted to get as far away from the sky as he possibly could. He found a pond and crawled into it. He swam down through the water to the pond's bottom and dug deep into the mud. Then he fell asleep. He slept all through the winter and didn't wake up until the spring. When he woke up, he was very proud of all the cracks still showing on his shell.

Ever since then, every turtle's shell has looked like it has cracks all over. And birds still fly south for the winter, but turtles pull their legs and heads into their shells, curl up, and sleep the winter away.

The End

Why Flies Buzz

ONE DAY A MAN and his wife went into the jungle to gather food. Along the way, they saw a tree that was full of delicious-looking coconuts. The man took off his shoes, grasped his knife in his right hand, and used his left hand to shimmy up to the very top of the tree to cut down some coconuts.

Take a Look

Does your child know what a jungle is? Read about jungle habitats in the Science chapter of this book. Use this illustration to talk about what kinds of plants grow in this jungle.

Use the Pictures

Help your child use the pictures in this story to visualize each episode in the story. After you read the words, retell the story again, pointing to parts of each picture.

As he did, a curious black fly flitted annoyingly around his face. "Stop that!" shouted the man, waving one arm to swat away the fly. But as he did so, the knife fell from his hand.

"Watch out, wife!" he cried. "I have dropped my knife!"

His frightened wife looked up just in time to see the knife tumbling toward her. She leapt out of its way— and kicked a long, green crocodile that had been dozing comfortably under the tree. Startled awake, and none too pleased, the crocodile gave three angry swats with his long, heavy tail— *swack! swack! swack!*

Nearby, a jungle bird was poking about in the grass, looking for beetles and bugs to eat. As the crocodile's tail came down, the bird squawked a terrified alarm—*scree! scree! scree!*

The bird soared to a branch in a nearby tree and landed right next to a monkey who had been quietly sitting, peeling the skin off a juicy mango. Disturbed by the sudden appearance of the panicky bird, the monkey dropped his mango. It fell down on the head of an unsuspecting hippo below—*splat! splat! splat!*

All Together

Encourage your child to make each animal sound with you as you read this story. After several readings, your child may be able to make the sounds all by herself.

Thinking that he was being attacked by hunters, the stunned hippo thrashed about wildly, trying to escape—*stomp! stomp! stomp!*

He trampled everything in his path, including a nest full of eggs that belonged to the bushfowl.

"My eggs are all broken!" wailed the mother bushfowl. She laid down next to her ruined nest and quietly began to cry—*sob! sob! sob!* And there she stayed for several days and several nights, not moving or making another sound.

Now in the jungle, a bushfowl acts very much like a rooster on a farm. Just as the rooster cock-a-doodle-doos each morning, the bushfowl rises early too. Her loud call—*kark! kark! kark!*—awakens the sun and starts each new day.

But now the bushfowl stayed silent, so sad was she over what had happened to her eggs. Because she did not call the sun, the sky remained dark for several days. The jungle animals became worried and went to seek the advice of the wise lion.

"Where is the sun, Lion?" they asked. "Why has there been no daylight for days?"

The lion gathered all the animals together. "Bushfowl," he said, "why have you stopped waking the sun each day?"

"Oh, wise lion," replied the bushfowl, "I am too sad to call the sun each day. I am sad because the hippo broke all the eggs in my nest."

Talk & Think

Pause here to be sure your child understands why the sky remained dark, without the sun, for days. If need be, read sentences over and talk about their meaning together.

"Ah hah," said the lion. "Then it is the hippo's fault. Hippo, why did you break all the eggs in the bushfowl's nest?"

"Wise lion," answered the hippo. "The monkey is to blame. She dropped a mango on my head, and I thought that hunters were attacking me."

"Ah hah," said the lion. "Then it is the monkey's fault!"

Talk & Think

As you read this part of the story, take time to help your child follow the lion's train of investigation. Each time the lion blames an animal, ask your child first if she thinks he is right. Then read how that animal responds.

"Wise lion, wise lion. Listen to me," said the monkey. "I only dropped the mango because the jungle bird swooped down beside me, shrieking loudly and frightening me."

"Ah hah," said the lion. "Then it is the jungle bird's fault!"

"It is not my fault," cried the bird. "The alligator swatted his tail in the grass next to me and scared me to death!"

"Ah hah," said the lion. "Then it is the alligator's fault!"

"Most certainly not," declared the alligator. "The woman kicked me and woke me from a peaceful nap!"

"Ah hah," said the lion. "Then the woman is to blame!"

"But, wise lion," cried the woman. "I was trying to get out of the way of the falling knife that my husband had dropped."

"Ah hah," said the lion. "Then it is the man's fault!"

"Wise lion," said the man, "I only dropped the knife because I was trying to swat away an annoying black fly that was flitting about my face."

"Ah hah," said the lion. "Then it is the black fly's fault!"

There was a long silence.

"Black fly," said the lion, "have you nothing to say?"

But instead of answering politely, as all the other animals had, the black fly just flew about their heads, saying *Buzz! Buzz! Buzz!* The lion repeated his question, but again the only reply that came from the fly was *Buzz! Buzz! Buzz!*

The lion frowned in anger. "Black fly!" he bellowed. "Since you refuse to answer and only wish to buzz, so be it! As punishment

for what you have done, I shall take away your power to talk. You will pass the rest of your days like this, just buzzing!"

The fly tried to speak in protest, but all he could say was *Buzz! Buzz! Buzz!* And to this day, flies all around the world say only *Buzz! Buzz! Buzz!*

As for the bushfowl, she was satisfied, for the one who had caused all the trouble from the start, the fly, had been punished. So she agreed, from the next morning on, to once again start every day by calling to the sun.

The End

The Lion and the Mouse

ONCE UPON A TIME there was a little mouse. He was scampering about among the trees and grass when quite by accident he happened to run across the paws of a large, sleeping lion. That woke the lion up from his afternoon nap.

As you might imagine, the lion was not at all pleased. He did not like to be awakened before he was ready!

Talk & Think
Before you turn the page, ask your child what you think might happen in this story. What will the lion say? What will the lion do? How do you think the mouse feels?

The lion reached out and angrily grabbed the mouse in his big paws. The lion was just about to eat him when the mouse cried out, "Please, kind sir, I didn't mean to disturb you. If you will let me go, I will be grateful to you forever. I promise that some day I will return your kindness by helping you."

The lion laughed out loud. "How in the world," he said, "could such a little animal as a mouse ever help so great an animal as a lion?" All the same, the lion decided to let the little mouse go.

Not long after, the mouse was once again running about among the same trees and grass when he heard a loud roar nearby. He moved closer to see who was making such a loud noise.

In a small clearing, he saw the very same lion trapped in a hunter's net. The lion roared ferociously as he struggled to free himself from the tangled web of ropes. But no matter how hard he struggled, he was not able to get loose from the hunter's trap.

Take a Look

You and your child can use these three pictures to talk about how the two animals feel at three very different moments. Ask your child to point to each picture and tell the story they tell together.

THE LION AND THE MOUSE

What About You?

Like all of Aesop's fables, this story teaches a lesson. Talk about the moral with your child. Find an example together in your own family or neighborhood that fits this moral.

The little mouse thought about running away. Those roars were so frightening! But he also remembered his promise to the lion. He had promised that if the lion let him go, he would return the kindness. He was a mouse who kept his promises, and so he thought very carefully and decided what to do.

He ran to the side of the great beast and started gnawing at the ropes of the net. He kept gnawing and gnawing with his sharp teeth until he finally made a hole in the net big enough so that the lion could escape.

The moral of this story is:
Friends who are little in size can
still be great friends.

The End

The City Mouse and the Country Mouse

ONCE UPON A TIME there were two mice who were cousins. One mouse lived in a small, simple house in the country. The other mouse lived in a large, stylish house in the city.

One day the City Mouse went to visit his cousin in the country. The Country Mouse was so happy to see the City Mouse,

Take a Look

Using the illustration above, talk about the differences between city and country. As possible, use examples from your own life. Do you live in a city or in the country?

Take a Look

Help your child name everything that the mice ate, as shown in the illustration. What would your child prefer to eat, the plain country food or the fancy city food?

he invited his cousin to stay with him at his country house and enjoy some dinner together.

The Country Mouse pulled two silver thimbles up to a spool of thread and used them as two chairs and a table. He set the table with two acorn caps and a little birthday cake candle.

He served a simple meal. They ate ripe peas from a pod and kernels of corn from a leftover can he had found in the barnyard.

As the two mice sat down, the City Mouse looked around, sniffed, and said, "Tut, tut! Oh my, oh my! Dear cousin, is this really dinner? How ever do you put up with such plain food?"

The Country Mouse answered, "My apologies, cousin, but this is what we eat every day in the country."

The City Mouse promptly invited the Country Mouse to come with him to his house in the city and be his guest for dinner. "Once you have tasted all the wonderful foods that we have in the city, you will never want to return to the country."

So the City Mouse and Country Mouse set off at once. They scampered through the fields and the neighborhoods and into the city. They arrived late that evening at the home of the City Mouse. The Country Mouse saw immediately that his cousin lived in a very grand house.

"Shhhh!" said the City Mouse as they entered the house through a little hole in the wall. "We must be careful to be sure that no one hears us!" The City Mouse led the way, looking right and left as he dashed through one large room after another. Finally, feeling safe, he waved his arm and invited his country cousin into a large dining room and up the leg of a huge dining table. The remains of somebody's magnificent feast still lay spread out on the table. They had left behind their silverware, their crystal glasses, their napkins—and a lot of their delicious food!

"Aren't you glad you joined me?" said the City Mouse. "This is how we eat every day in the city."

The Country Mouse could hardly believe it. There was a big fat ham, with lots of meat left on the bone. There were bowls with bits of sweet potatoes and broccoli still in them. There were crumbs and slices of a delicious chocolate cake with white icing left behind, along with apple cores, orange peels, and a few bunches of grapes. There were bowls of jam, plates of cheese, and slices of bread—food enough for an entire mouse family! There was more food than the Country Mouse had ever seen before.

New Words

Ask your child what she thinks it means that the City Mouse lived in a "grand house." "Grand" means both big and fancy.

"Magnificent" is another word meaning big and fancy.

A "feast" is a big, special meal. Ask your child for his idea of a meal that could be called a magnificent feast.

The two mice got busy, nibbling away. "Delicious," munched the Country Mouse appreciatively. "I have never eaten such fine food." Then both mice stopped in the middle of a bite. They heard loud growls, snarls, and hisses coming at them.

"Quick! Follow me!" yelled the City Mouse.

He scampered to the floor, with his cousin right behind him, just as two huge dogs and an angry-looking cat raced into the dining room. The two mice ran for their lives! They escaped just in time, dashing through a small hole in the wall.

Talk & Think

Why are there cake crumbs and apple cores on the table? Be sure your child understands that the mice are eating leftovers after people have eaten and gone away. Remind him of the can of corn in the country. Both mice serve meals made of people's leftovers.

New Words

Does your child know what the City Mouse means when he says "That was close"? It means that danger came very near, but they escaped safely. Maybe your child can find times in daily life to say "That was close!"

"Whew! That was close," said the City Mouse. "We'll wait here until they leave, and then we can finish our meal."

But the Country Mouse was so frightened, he couldn't even talk. He had never been in such danger before. He thought back to his own simple house in the country and realized how much better he liked it there. He decided that it was time to go home. He did not even say goodbye to his cousin. The Country Mouse picked up his belongings and scampered out of the city house. He ran all the way home to the country, where he felt safe and sound and happy.

The moral of the story is: Sometimes the plainest and simplest things are still better than the richest and finest.

The End

History

■ Young children spend most of their time immersed in the day-to-day events of an immediate world of family, home, friends, and community. Yet preschoolers naturally seek to broaden that world, and early lessons about history can capitalize on that curiosity.

These nonfiction read-alouds offer well-known stories—legendary or factual—from the history of the United States. Each read-aloud says something important about the character and ideals of this nation. By sharing them, you can broaden your child's understanding of the world, as well as his sense of time, of the past, and of his relationship to the past.

Treat these readings as if they were stories, not accounts to be memorized. For now, the goal is for your child to grasp the idea that real people lived in times gone by.

The First Americans

THE COUNTRY WHERE we live is called the United States of America.
It did not always look the way it looks today.

Many, many, many years ago—long before your mother and
father were born, long before your grandparents were born, long
before even their mothers and fathers were born—four hundred

years ago, America looked very different. There were no houses like the ones we have today. There were no stores, no other buildings, no cars, no telephones, no televisions.

Instead, there were forests thick with many trees. There were grassy fields, lakes and rivers, and many animals. There were furry animals in the forest, birds in the trees and in the skies, and fish in the lakes and rivers. There were also some people living long ago in this land. These people were the first people to live in America. So we call them Native Americans or American Indians.

The American Indians lived simply, eating fish that they caught, animals that they hunted, plants and berries that they found growing wild. They also planted seeds in the ground and grew vegetables like corn and squash to eat.

In those days long ago, some people who were living in another country, far away from America, decided that they wanted to move away from their homes. They lived in a country called England. A king ruled England. He made many rules that told people how they must live. He even told them what church they should attend. It made many people unhappy. They did not like the king telling them what to do or think. They wanted to live somewhere else.

Then and Now
Talk with your child about the picture. What does it look like this man is doing? How can you tell this picture shows a time long ago? Who do you think this man is?

Sailing to America

So some people in England decided to move to another land. They did not know very much about America or the Indians who lived there. They did know that it was far away from England and the king. So they all got on a small ship, named the *Mayflower*, and started to sail across the Atlantic Ocean.

Take a Look

Talk about the picture of the *Mayflower*. Find a picture of a modern ship and help your child understand how the *Mayflower* was different from a modern ship.

It was a difficult trip. It took many months to sail from England to America. The people on the ship were crowded together. They sailed through stormy weather. There was not enough food for everyone. Some people got very sick. Everyone on the ship was glad to get to the end of the journey.

These people who sailed to America were called the Pilgrims. When they arrived, they looked around and saw a place so different from anything they had seen before. There were no houses like their homes in England. The people they met, the Indians, did not look or talk like them at all.

New American Friends

Many of the Pilgrims felt discouraged. They were all working hard, but life was still very difficult. They did not know how to live in this land that was so new and strange to them. Some of them became sick and died.

Take a Look

Talk about the people in the picture. Ask your child to point to the Native American. Where are the Pilgrims? The Mayflower? How do you think the different people in the picture feel?

One day, some Pilgrims met a Native American man whose name was Squanto. Squanto had lived all his life in America. He knew all about the forests, lakes, and rivers. He knew how to find and grow food. Best of all, he knew how to speak some English, so the Pilgrims could talk with him.

Squanto became friends with the Pilgrims. He showed them how to hunt turkey and deer in the forest. He showed them how to catch fish in the streams. He showed them where to find wild greens and sweet berries. Squanto also showed the Pilgrims which plants grew well in American soil. They had never seen or tasted corn or squash. They were amazed and thankful when Squanto showed them these new plants.

With Squanto's help, the Pilgrims soon had enough food. Fewer people became sick, and their lives grew happier. They saved some of the food that grew in the summer so they would still have something to eat when it became cold in the winter.

Talk & Think
After you have read this section, ask your child to tell you how Squanto helped the Pilgrims.

An American Holiday

After summer was over, the Pilgrims felt that it was time to celebrate. They wanted to thank God and the Indians for helping them learn how to live in their new home. This party, or celebration, was the first Thanksgiving in America.

The Indians came to the party with the Pilgrims. They had a wonderful feast, with plenty of food for everyone. They ate turkey and deer they had hunted in the woods, fish they had caught in the rivers, and corn and squash they had grown. They played games and told stories. Their party lasted three days!

The first Thanksgiving happened many, many years ago, but people who live in the United States of America still enjoy celebrating. Thanksgiving has become a national holiday, a special time to get together with friends and family. Americans often share a special Thanksgiving dinner with others, remembering how the Indians and Pilgrims shared food together, too.

Then & Now
Talk about what these people are doing. Does your family celebrate Thanksgiving? How is your family's Thanksgiving different than the first Thanksgiving? How is it the same?

George Washington and the Cherry Tree

Do It Yourself

Show your child a U.S. one-dollar bill and talk about whose face is shown on it. Come back to it after your child knows this story.

A LONG TIME AGO—many, many, many years ago—long before your mother and father were born, long before your grandmother and grandfather were born, and long before even their mothers and fathers were born, more than two hundred years ago—a boy named George Washington lived in America. George lived on a farm with his mother and father. There were horses, pigs, and cows

110

on the farm. There were fields planted full of corn and tobacco and an orchard with many fruit trees. George's father, Mr. Washington, was fond of his fruit trees, especially a young cherry tree that he had received as a gift.

George's New Hatchet

There is a famous story about George Washington and this cherry tree. People have told the story for many, many years. Nowadays we know that somebody made up the story and that it didn't really happen. But the story shows what kind of person George Washington was, even as a boy, so we still like to tell it.

When George was a small boy, his father gave him a brand new hatchet. George was delighted. He tried using his new hatchet on logs from the woodpile: *chop, chop, chop!*

Then a thought came to him. Wouldn't it be exciting to cut down a real tree?

So George Washington went into his father's orchard. He saw a fine young tree, and he set to work with his new hatchet. *chop, chop, chop! Crash!* The tree fell to the ground.

George was proud to see how well his new hatchet chopped. He looked at the tree, lying on the ground, and only then did he realize that this was a very special cherry tree, given to his father as a gift. George had chopped down that special cherry tree, and now the tree would die.

"I Cannot Tell a Lie"

Soon George's father came home. He had been thinking about the big, juicy cherries that were growing sweeter every day on his favorite cherry tree. He went into the orchard, hoping to pick a handful of ripe cherries and taste those sweet fruits.

But when he got to the orchard, he couldn't believe what he saw. There was his favorite cherry tree, lying on the ground. Mr. Washington asked one person after another, "Who chopped down my cherry tree?"

Everyone shook his head. No one knew. Finally Mr. Washington came to his son, young George.

George knew he had done something wrong. He had not been thinking when he chopped down that tree. He felt ashamed. He also felt scared, because he knew his father was angry.

"George," said Mr. Washington, "do you know who cut down my cherry tree?"

George looked up into his father's angry eyes. He took a deep breath. He did not look away. He said, "Father, I cannot tell a lie. I cut down the cherry tree."

"I was looking forward to eating cherries from that tree," his father said sternly.

"I am sorry," said young George.

"I am sorry, too, George," said his father, "but it is good that you told me the truth. I would rather lose a cherry tree than have you tell a lie."

What About You?
Ask your child how George must have felt when his father asked him who chopped down the cherry tree. Ask, "Have you ever felt like that?"

The First President

When George Washington grew up, he became the first president of the United States of America. Many people call him "the Father of Our Country," because he did so much to help get it started. George Washington worked hard to help the United States. He was honest all his life. He was not afraid to face difficulties. He was the kind of person Americans admire.

When we tell the story of the cherry tree, we remember George Washington, the boy who grew up to be our first president. We also think about how important it is to be honest, no matter how hard it might be.

Take a Look
Use the picture below to talk with your child about Washington, D.C. "It is the capital of the United States. The president and other people who lead our country work there." Talk about where the city gets its name.

Betsy Ross and the American Flag

Then & Now

It's hard to imagine life long ago. Use the painting above and the photograph opposite, Betsy Ross's house in Philadelphia today, to talk about life in centuries past.

A LONG TIME AGO—many, many years ago, long before your mother and father were born, long before your grandmother and grandfather were born, and long before even your grandparents' mothers and fathers were born—more than two hundred years ago—there lived a girl whose name was Betsy Ross.

Betsy Ross went to school every day. She learned to read and write and do arithmetic, just as you and other children do today. She also learned something else at school. She learned to sew. Betsy and all the other girls in her school practiced sewing every day. They learned how to sew with a needle and thread. No one had a sewing machine back then.

Betsy Ross's Shop

Betsy Ross became very good at sewing. When she grew up, she married a man who built furniture. They worked together. He would build the wooden part of a chair or sofa, and she would sew the fabric to cover the seat. She sewed cushions and curtains as well. People came from near and far to the little shop in the city of Philadelphia where Betsy Ross and her husband sold the furniture they made. One day, some important visitors came to Betsy Ross's shop. One of the visitors was George Washington.

Talk & Think
Turn back to the story just before this one to help your child remember George Washington.

"Betsy Ross, we have an important job for you," said George Washington. "We want you to sew a flag—a flag for this new country that we are helping to plan. We need a flag for the United States of America."

George Washington and his friends talked with Betsy Ross about the new country's flag. "Let's use bright colors. How about red, white, and blue?" suggested Betsy.

They liked that idea. "I could make stars with five points out of white cloth," said Betsy. "I could sew those white stars onto a square of blue cloth." They liked that idea, too.

"For the rest of the flag, I could make red and white stripes, sewn together. A flag like that would look good, flying in the wind. It would show that we are proud of our country."

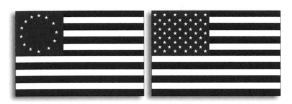

Then & Now
The flag on the left is the one designed by Betsy Ross. The flag on the right is today's. Help your child point to what is different and what is the same about the two flags.

Betsy Ross sewed a flag with the design she had described. She showed it to George Washington and his friends. They liked it. That was the first flag of the United States of America.

Our Flag Today

It has been a long time since Betsy Ross sewed that first flag for George Washington. Since then, the United States flag has changed many times, but it still has the design that Betsy Ross showed George Washington.

Today, the flag of the United States of America has red and white stripes, and it has white stars on a rectangle of blue, just as Betsy Ross designed it more than two hundred years ago. But today there are many more stars on our flag than there were on the flag sewn by Betsy Ross.

Do It Yourself
Look together for flags in your everyday life. When you see one, ask your child to remember and tell you the story of Betsy Ross.

The American flag still looks bright and strong, flying in the wind. It still reminds us that we are proud of our country, the United States of America.

Abraham Lincoln, Log Cabin President

MORE THAN one hundred years ago—before your mother and father, your grandmother and grandfather, and even their parents were born—a boy named Abraham Lincoln grew up in America. People called him by his nickname: "Abe."

Take a Look

Ask your child what the picture tells about the man in the story, even before reading it.

Abe Lincoln's family lived in a little log cabin all by itself far out in the country. His family cut down trees to make a place in the woods, then they used those logs to build the cabin.

Abe's family was not rich, and he had to work hard every day. He helped his father with the farm. He planted seeds and plowed the field. He split wood to make fences and chopped wood for the fire. He spent so much time working, he could not go to school.

But Abe still loved learning. At night, he was so tired after working outside all day, but he stayed awake, teaching himself how to read. In those days long ago, no one had electric lights that they could turn on to make light at night. So in order to read, Abe sat next to the fireplace. The light from the fire helped him see the words on the pages of the books he was reading.

Take a Look

Help your child learn what a log cabin is by talking about this replica at the Lincoln Boyhood National Memorial in Indiana. "Is it big or small? How many windows can you see? Do you see the chimney? Would you like to live here?"

The Rewards of Hard Work

As Abe got older, he continued to work very hard, helping his father during the day and studying books at night. He read as many books as he could find. Once Abe borrowed a book from a neighbor. It rained that night, and the cabin roof leaked. The book Abe had borrowed got all wet. It was ruined.

Abe Lincoln was an honest boy. He carried the ruined book back to his neighbor. "Our roof leaked, and the rain came in on your book," he admitted. "I am so sorry. What can I do to repay you?" They agreed that Abe would work for three whole days in his neighbor's fields in order to pay for the book that had been ruined.

As he grew up, more and more people came to admire Abe Lincoln for his honesty and his willingness to work hard. They elected him the sixteenth president of the United States. Many believe he was one of the greatest of all the American presidents.

President Lincoln and Slavery

Abraham Lincoln was president at a time when there was a war between the people who lived in the states located in the North and the people who lived in the states located in the South.

People in the South had great, big farms, called plantations. They grew crops like cotton and tobacco to make money.

The farms were so big, they needed lots of people to work on them. Ships sailed across the ocean from Africa, bringing people to

Do It Yourself
Show your child a penny and help him find Lincoln's face. Play a game and find all the features shared by the silhouette on the penny and the portrait above.

America. The African people did not want to come. They wanted to stay home, but they were forced to come to work as slaves.

Farmers in the South made the African slaves work on their plantations. The slaves had to do whatever the farmers told them. They did not get paid for their work. They were not allowed to leave the plantation or to go live anywhere else.

Back then, people in the United States did not agree about whether it was right for people to have slaves. Many people in the North thought it was a bad idea. They wanted to make a rule against having slaves. But many people in the South wanted slaves to work on their plantations. They wanted to follow different rules. The people in the South and the people in the North went to war against each other over these disagreements.

During the war, Abraham Lincoln said no one in the United States of America could have slaves anymore. When the war ended, people in the North and in the South agreed to follow the same rules and stay together as one country: the United States of America.

Take a Look

Show your child the Lincoln Memorial, below, built in the city of Washington, D.C. "The statue sits inside the building. Can you see it in both pictures?"

Martin Luther King, Jr.,
A Man of Peace

NOT VERY long ago—probably about the same time that your grandmother was a little girl and your grandfather was a little boy—a young boy named Martin was growing up in the United States. His full name was Martin Luther King, Jr.

Take a Look

Look together at this picture of Martin Luther King, Jr. Ask your child where she thinks it might have been taken.

Separate Ways in Days Gone By

Other children lived in the neighborhood, right next door to Martin's house, but their mothers and fathers would not let them play with Martin. Martin and his family were black people, African Americans. The other families in their neighborhood were white people.

The white families would not let their children play with Martin and his brother and sister because their skin color was different. The white children did not even go to school with the King children. The white parents sent their children to a school just for white children, while Martin and his brother and sister went to a school just for black children.

Martin did not think it was fair. Black children and white children should go to the same school. As he grew up, he learned about other ways in which black people and white people lived separately from each other in America.

In those days, nearly everywhere, black people were treated differently from white people. They could not use the same bathrooms. They could not drink at the same

Take a Look

Above, Martin Luther King, Jr.'s house when he was a boy. Below, a classroom from those times. Talk with your child about what she sees in these pictures.

water fountains. They could not eat in the same restaurants or stay at the same hotels. When black people got on a bus, sometimes the driver told them they had to sit in seats in the back. Only white people were allowed to ride in front.

Martin Luther King grew up and went to college. He decided to become a minister at a church. He wanted to help change things so that all people in America, no matter whether they were black or white or other colors, were treated fairly.

Martin Luther King, Jr., talked to many people, black and white, rich and poor. He could see how many of them were feeling angry about how differently black and white people lived in the United States.

Some black people were angry because they

Talk & Think
To get a sense of how well your child is understanding, ask, "What was it that Martin Luther King, Jr., wanted to change in the United States of America?"

wanted things to change quickly. Some white people were angry because they did not want things to change at all. People started to fight, and some people got hurt. Other people wanted the government to help make laws that could change the country and make it a good place for everyone to live.

Martin Luther King, Jr., traveled far and wide. He made many speeches, talking to crowds of people wherever he went. He asked people to stop fighting. He always said that people should be fair and find ways to change things peacefully.

Martin Luther King's Dream

Martin Luther King, Jr. was a man of peace. He knew that in order to get your way, it was better to use words and kind behavior than to shout, argue, or fight.

In a famous speech, Martin Luther King, Jr., said, "I have a dream." His dream was that black children and white children would "walk together as sisters and brothers." People listened. They liked the dream that Martin Luther King, Jr., described. They wanted to work together to make it come true.

Today, children of all colors go to school together. We share water fountains, restaurants, and hotels. It is still good to remember the words and ideas of Martin Luther King, Jr., which help us live together peacefully.

Talk About It

Are there children of different races in your neighborhood or town? Do they play peacefully together? Reading about Dr. King can give you a chance to talk about race with your child.

Then & Now

Invite your child to look at this picture of a school classroom today, then turn back the page and look at the one from the time when Martin Luther King, Jr., was a boy. What is the same in the two classrooms? What is different?

Science

Science means learning about the world. For a preschooler, that learning begins with casual experiences and observations. An adult can enrich those learning moments by offering coherence and structure.

Start by setting the example of thinking about things the way a scientist would. Talk about what your child already knows about a realm of the natural world, like plants or insects. Jot down her comments, then ask what she still wonders about—what she would like to learn about these things. Write down her remarks as questions. Next, start investigating!

The nonfiction read-aloud selections here provide starting points for conversations about the living and physical worlds. Always arrange for plenty of hands-on discovery as well, so that your child can observe, experiment, and try things out in person.

After all your reading and explorations, take the time to help your child summarize what she has learned.

Animals Are Living Things

Do It Yourself

Make a scrapbook of animals your child knows in her daily life: pets, animals including birds that you see outside every day, animals she enjoys at the zoo. Remind her, "These are all animals."

WORMS AND WHALES, beetles and bears, bunnies and kittens, goldfish and snails—what do they all have in common? They are all animals. You are an animal, too.

Animals are alive. They can have babies. Baby animals grow up and become adult animals. Then they have babies of their own. Animals can move around. Often they move around to find something to eat.

Animals have different kinds of bodies

Animals come in all sizes and shapes. Some animals are smaller than your thumbnail. Think of how small an ant is! Some animals are huge. A blue whale is as long as three fire trucks.

We put animals in groups, depending on how their bodies are shaped and the ways they live. Here are some animal groups to read about. Let's talk about the shape of their bodies.

Take a Look
Together with your child, count the legs on this ant. Point out the difference between legs and antennae. How many legs? Is it an insect or a spider?

Insects and spiders. Insects and spiders are tiny. There are millions of different kinds of them. Insects all have six legs. Spiders all have eight legs. Some insects have wings and fly. Some do not.

Take a Look
Like the insects, this animal has two antennae in front. Help your child point to its head. Now count the legs together. Is it an insect or a spider?

Take a Look
Count the body parts of the two insects, first the ant and then the beetle. It is easier to see the three separate parts on the ant. Help your child see them on the beetle, too.

Birds. Birds are animals that have wings and feathers. Wings and feathers help birds fly. Birds can walk, too.

Take a Look
This bird is using wings to fly in the air. Help your child find two wings. How many legs does this bird have? It can walk, too.

Fish. Fish are animals that live underwater. They have fins and tails. They flap their fins and wave their tails to move and swim through the water. They find their food underwater.

Do It Yourself
Has your child ever gone fishing? Or maybe your child has seen fish in the market or on the dinner table. Explain that we catch fish and eat them. The fish in this photo are alive. You can visit a pet shop together to see live fish up close.

What About You?
Ask your child how it would feel to touch this friendly lizard's skin. Dry, bumpy, tough. Count the toes on the lizard's front foot together.

What About You?
Ask your child how it would feel to touch this frog's skin. Smooth and slippery. The spots on this frog protect it. When it hides in the weeds, other animals can't see it.

Reptiles and amphibians. Snakes and lizards are called reptiles. Reptiles are animals that can live in dry places. Frogs and toads are called amphibians. Amphibians must live near water. Frogs live in water some of the time and on land some of the time.

Mammals. Mammals are animals with warm bodies. They grow hair on their bodies. The hair, or fur, that they grow on their bodies helps to keep them warm.

Some mammals walk on four legs. Some mammals walk on two legs. Some mammals use their arms or even their tails to balance and move around.

Mother mammals make milk with their bodies. Baby mammals drink their mothers' milk.

Talk & Think

Help your child decide if cats are mammals. Do they have hair or fur? What are these baby kittens doing? They are drinking milk from their mother. That must mean that a cat is a mammal.

130

Animals move in different ways

All animal use the parts of their bodies to move. Different kinds of animal bodies move in different ways. Dogs run on four legs. Monkeys have two strong arms and two strong legs. Sometimes they use their arms to swing from tree to tree in the air, and sometimes they use their legs to walk on the ground. Can you think of an animal that moves with no legs? Snakes and worms have no legs, but they move very well.

Talk & Think
Ask your child how many legs he uses when he runs. How many legs does this dog use when he runs? What other animals use four legs for moving? There are lots of right answers!

Take a Look
Talk about how this monkey is using both arms and legs to climb. Talk about times when your child used four limbs for moving, too—starting with when she crawled.

Animals have ways to protect themselves

New Words

What does it mean to say an animal "protects" itself? It means that whenever that animal feels afraid, it has a way to keep itself from getting hurt.

Many animals have bodies that help protect them from getting hurt. Some have sharp teeth or sharp claws. Some have strong legs that they can use for kicking or for running away.

Turtles have hard shells outside and soft bodies inside. The shells keep their bodies inside from getting hurt.

Skunks have a different way to keep from getting hurt. They can make a bad smell with their bodies and spray it at other animals. That makes other animals stay away.

132

Animals eat plants or other animals

Wild animals spend a lot of time looking for food. Different creatures eat different kinds of food. Some, such as cows or grasshoppers, eat only plants. Animals that eat only plants are called herbivores. Other animals, such as lions or wolves, eat only other animals. Animals that eat other animals are called carnivores. Many animals, like raccoons and chickens, eat both. Animals that eat plants and other animals are called omnivores.

Talk & Think
Talk more to your child about food for animals. When animals are pets, or when animals live in zoos or on farms, people give them food. But wild animals must find their own food.

Take a Look
This bird, called an egret, is eating a fish. It also eats insects and even small birds. It does not eat plants. Is it an herbivore, a carnivore, or an omnivore?

Animals grow up and change as they grow

New Words

Help your child learn the words for baby animals. Baby cats are kittens, baby dogs are puppies, baby ducks are ducklings, baby chickens are chicks. Find pictures in books or magazines and practice using these words.

Every animal grows from little to big, from baby to grown-up. First the animal is born. It grows bigger and becomes an adult. Then it has babies of its own.

After it grows up, every animal dies. Some animals go all the way from birth to death in just a few days. Other animals live to be one hundred years old.

How a cat grows

When kittens are born, they are teeny-tiny, no bigger than your hand. When they grow up, cats look a lot like they did when they were kittens, only bigger.

How a frog grows

1 First, the mother frog lays frog **eggs** in the water.

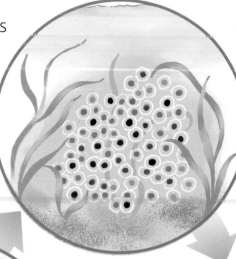

2 Then **tadpoles** hatch from the eggs. Tadpoles have long tails and swim in the water. Tadpoles grow up to be frogs.

4 As a tadpole becomes a **frog**, it looks very different. Now it has no tail. It has four strong legs. It uses those legs to walk and jump on land—and to swim in the water, too.

3 As tadpoles grow, their bodies change. Their tails shrink. Legs grow from their bodies. They still swim in the water.

Some animals live and work together

Talk & Think
What work do animals do? They make homes, like birds' nests. They find and store food. They raise babies. Find more examples together.

Some animals always live with others of their kind. Ants are one kind of animal that lives and works together. Many ants live together. Every ant has its own special job. Have you ever seen an ant marching across the ground? It had a job to do.

An ant colony

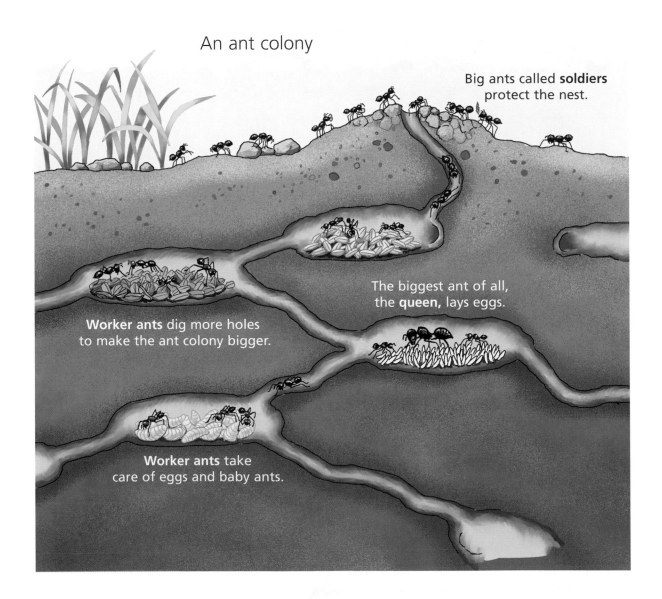

Big ants called **soldiers** protect the nest.

The biggest ant of all, the **queen**, lays eggs.

Worker ants dig more holes to make the ant colony bigger.

Worker ants take care of eggs and baby ants.

Take a Look
You can use this owl as an example of an animal that lives in a habitat called a forest. Ask your child what else is in this picture with the owl. The trees are part of the forest habitat. The owl lives in the trees.

Animals live in different habitats

Every animal has a place where it likes to live the most. The place where an animal lives is called that animal's habitat.

Deer, raccoons, squirrels, blue jays, and ants live in the forest with this owl. Many plants and animals can share the same habitat. In the right habitat, plants and animals find everything they need to live and grow: food, water, and a place to live.

The farm. A farm is a habitat where certain kinds of plants and animals live. The farmer takes care of the plants, such as corn and grass, that grow in the fields of the farm. The animals that live on the farm—like cows, horses, and pigs—eat the corn and grass. The plants and the animals share the farm habitat and live well together.

New Words
Many farms, like this one, have a building called a barn, where animals sleep at night and where farmers keep equipment like tractors. Many farms also have a barnyard, like this one: an area with a fence around it, where animals can stay outside but will not run away.

The desert. A desert habitat is very dry. It hardly ever rains in the desert. Days are often very hot. Nights can be very cold. Desert plants can grow for a long time without needing much water. In many deserts, the ground is made of sand, not soil.

The python is a snake that lives in the desert. It doesn't need much water, and its body stays comfortable no matter whether the air is very hot or very cold. Those are two reasons why this snake lives in a desert habitat.

The ocean. Many plants and animals live in the habitat called the ocean. It is the biggest habitat on Earth. Ocean water is salty—too salty for you to drink. Plants and animals in the ocean habitat do well in salty water.

The shark is a large fish that lives in the ocean. It spends its whole life underwater. It swims with its fins and tail. It eats other animals. Sharks have gills on the sides of their heads that let them breathe underwater.

Talk & Think

Sharks eat other animals that they find in the ocean. They like to eat other fish. They do not eat any plants at all. So is a shark a herbivore, a carnivore, or an omnivore?

140

The jungle. In a jungle habitat, the air is warm and moist. It rains almost every day. It never gets cold enough for snow. Lots of plants grow in the jungle. Big trees grow close together, their trunks standing tall and their branches stretching up toward the sky. Long vines hang from one tree to another.

The toucan is a bird that lives in the jungle habitat. It eats fruit and insects. It grabs them with its big beak.

Lots of other animals live in the jungle habitat, like monkeys and snakes—but the kinds of snakes living in a jungle are different from those that live in a desert habitat.

Talk & Think

Help your child figure out the answer to this question: What part of the body does this toucan use to move? It can either walk or fly.

Humans Are
Special Animals

Talk & Think

Help your child compare humans with other animals. All have ears, a nose, a mouth, and eyes. But do other animals smile for the camera? Do they laugh and joke? Do they talk?

PEOPLE ARE ANIMALS—a special kind of animal called a human being. Like other animals, human beings have bodies that move around. They eat food and drink water. Humans are born. They grow up and have babies. When they get old, they die. All your friends and the people in your family are humans.

142

In some ways, human beings are different from other animals. We have brains that we use when we think, feel, and learn. Humans can talk. We stand on two legs and use our hands to hold onto things.

Humans are adaptable

Human beings make their homes in places all over the world. They live in almost every sort of habitat. Some humans live where it is hot and dry. Others live where it is cold and icy. We humans can live in a jungle where it rains often or in a desert where it almost never rains.

What about other habitats? Humans live on farms. Humans build houses in forests. How about the ocean? Some humans live on boats. Some explore underwater, but they don't live there.

New Words
"Adaptable" means able to change. Humans can live in many different habitats because they can make changes in the way they live.

Take a Look
The people below live in two very different habitats: hot and dry, cold and icy. Talk together about how they have adapted.

Humans have amazing bodies

Do It Yourself

Have fun exploring these body facts. Read through each of the descriptions of body parts below and ask your child to act them out as you read them.

Just think of all the parts that make up the human body! You can see some parts on the outside, like legs, arms, eyes, nose, and mouth. Many other parts are hidden inside. On the outside, people may look different, one from another. But their bodies, outside and inside, all work just about the same way.

What's outside?

Your arms help you keep balance.

You use your hands to touch and hold things.

Your legs help you walk, run, and jump.

You stand on your feet.

Inside your body, under your skin, lots of things are happening all the time. You can't see them, and sometimes you can't even feel them, but there are many parts inside your body that help you move and eat, breathe and think.

What's inside?

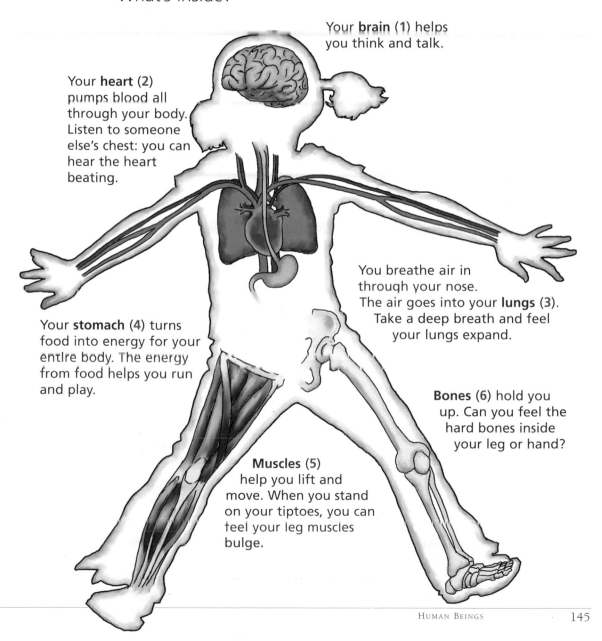

Your **brain** (1) helps you think and talk.

Your **heart** (2) pumps blood all through your body. Listen to someone else's chest: you can hear the heart beating.

You breathe air in through your nose. The air goes into your **lungs** (3). Take a deep breath and feel your lungs expand.

Your **stomach** (4) turns food into energy for your entire body. The energy from food helps you run and play.

Bones (6) hold you up. Can you feel the hard bones inside your leg or hand?

Muscles (5) help you lift and move. When you stand on your tiptoes, you can feel your leg muscles bulge.

Humans use five senses

Humans use special parts of their bodies to learn about the world around them. We learn about the world by seeing, hearing, smelling, tasting, and touching things in it. These are called the five senses. Which senses are you using now? For each of the five senses, you use a different part of your body.

The five senses

With your **vision**, or sight, you look at things.

Another sense tells how things **smell**.

When you **hear**, you take in sound and understand it.

Taste tells you if food is sweet, salty, sour, or bitter.

You use the sense of **touch** to learn how things feel.

Talk & Think

Help your child talk about all the ways that adults take care of babies. They feed them, wash them, and put clothes on them. They keep them warm and dry. Later, adults teach babies to walk and talk.

Humans have babies

Human mothers give birth to human babies. Like many other animal babies, human babies are pretty helpless when they are first born. They can't talk or walk. They can't find their own food or water. They can't put on their clothes by themselves.

Parents take care of children as they grow. As humans grow older, they learn how to talk and walk. Then they learn how to read and write. By about the age of twenty years old, humans have grown up and they can take care of themselves.

How old are you? Think about all the things that you can do now that you couldn't do when you were a baby.

Humans want to stay healthy

Like other animals, humans need to eat food and drink plenty of water. Humans are omnivores. They cook and eat meat that they get from animals. They eat food from plants, too.

Humans need to keep themselves clean and safe. One important part of growing up is learning all the things a person should do to stay healthy.

Ways to stay healthy

Eat healthful **food**

Drink **water**

Get enough **sleep**

Stay **warm** and **dry**

Brush **teeth** often

Stay **clean** by washing your hands and taking baths

Exercise to keep your body strong

Follow good **safety habits**, like:

Look both ways before crossing the street

Wear a safety helmet when on skates, skateboard, or bike

Be careful around knives, stoves, and fire

Wear sunscreen when you're out in bright sunshine

Plants Are Living Things

PLANTS DON'T MOVE AROUND or make sounds the way animals do, but plants are alive. They need food and water. They start small and grow bigger. Then they make more little plants.

Unlike animals, plants stay in one place. They need sunlight, water, soil, and air. With those, they make their food.

Do It Yourself
Do you have house-plants or a garden nearby? You can look at those and talk about them while you read this section together. Preschoolers always learn more from real-life examples.

There are many different kinds of plants

Do It Yourself
Talk a walk together and see how many different kinds of plants you can find. Don't forget grass, weeds, potted plants, and trees.

Plants come in all shapes and sizes. Trees and bushes, all sorts of flowers, grass, weeds, and vegetables—all of these are plants. Some plants are smaller than your thumbnail. Others, like the giant sequoia tree, grow higher than tall buildings.

Plants grow all around the world. They grow in places where they can find light and water. Like animals, different plants have different habitats. Some grow in the jungle, where it is moist and warm. Others live in the desert, where it is hot and dry. Some plants even live in the ocean.

Plants have different parts

Green plants have five basic body parts: roots, stem, leaves, flowers, and seeds. Seeds sprout into new plants.

The parts of a sunflower

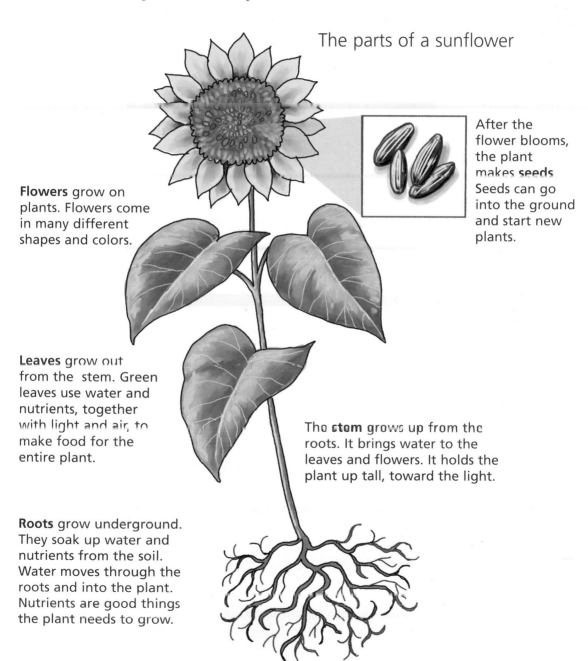

Flowers grow on plants. Flowers come in many different shapes and colors.

After the flower blooms, the plant makes **seeds** Seeds can go into the ground and start new plants.

Leaves grow out from the stem. Green leaves use water and nutrients, together with light and air, to make food for the entire plant.

The **stem** grows up from the roots. It brings water to the leaves and flowers. It holds the plant up tall, toward the light.

Roots grow underground. They soak up water and nutrients from the soil. Water moves through the roots and into the plant. Nutrients are good things the plant needs to grow.

Most plants start growing from seeds

Talk & Think
What seeds do we eat? Corn, peas, and beans are seeds. Nuts are seeds. Grains like wheat are seeds that we grind into flour.

Plants grow from seeds. Most seeds grow inside flowers. Seeds can also grow inside cones, like those on a pine tree.

Fruits grow around seeds. Have you ever seen the seeds inside an apple? Have you found seeds inside an orange or a grapefruit? How about the little seeds in a banana?

Nuts are seeds, too. They grow inside shells or husks.

Fruit and nuts

Your kitchen will have many examples of seeds. Slice through an apple, crack open a peanut shell, or look inside other fruits or nuts to find the seed. It's fine to eat seeds. They will never sprout inside you!

An apple is a fruit with seeds inside.

A peanut is a nut that grows inside a shell.

Plants go through stages as they grow

Plants start as seeds. They grow into plants. They flower and make more seeds. Then the cycle begins again.

How a pea plant grows

5 Pea **seeds** grow inside the pods. We can plant the seeds, and the cycle begins again. Or we can eat the seeds—yum! Green peas!

1 A **seed** starts growing in the soil.

2 A **sprout** grows up out of the seed. Roots grow down out of the seed.

3 The plant gets bigger and grows **leaves**.

4 Then the plant grows **flowers**. Pea **pods** grow from inside the flowers.

Plants make food for people

Do It Yourself

Talk about what your child has eaten today. Which foods came from plants? Find pictures in magazines or books to show the plants that those foods come from.

In gardens and on farms, people grow plants to eat. Farmers work hard in their fields to care for plants such as wheat, corn, peas, beans, apples, strawberries, and tomatoes. When the plants are grown, the farmers gather them from the fields.

Farmers send some plants, like wheat, to factories to be made into foods, like bread and cereal. They send other plants, like lettuce and carrots, straight to the grocery store for people to buy. Next time you go to the grocery store, think about the farmers who grew these fruits and vegetables for you!

Plants are important in our world

Plants are important to people for another reason, too. Plants make oxygen, an important part of the air we breathe. Humans need plants to be able to breathe and stay alive and healthy.

Plants and animals, including humans, need each other.

Talk & Think

As you read, it's a good idea to pause now and then and talk together about all your child is learning. Take the time now to talk about plants and animals. How are they the same? How are they different from one another?

Talk & Think

Nearly three-quarters of
a child's weight is made
up of water. Divide your
child's weight by 8 —
that's how many gallons
of water are in his body!

Water Is Important

WITHOUT WATER, there would be no life on Earth. Plants and animals
need to take in water to survive. So it's good that water covers most
of our planet. It fills our oceans, lakes and ponds, rivers and
streams. Water flows underground, and water floats in the clouds.

Water can take different forms

We can find different forms of water. Most of the time, we think of water as a liquid. Water is liquid in puddles, rivers, lakes, and ponds. Water running from a hose or faucet is liquid.

When it gets very cold or very hot, water can change form and it isn't liquid anymore.

When water gets very cold, it changes into solid ice. A frozen pond on a cold winter day or ice cubes from the freezer are both examples of water in a solid form.

When water gets very hot, it changes into steam, a gas. Sometimes on a hot day, after it has rained, you can see steam rising from puddles or ponds. You can also see water turn to steam when you cook it on a hot stove.

Take a Look
This boy is skating on water! Help your child decide whether the ice is water in the form of solid, liquid, or gas. Water is both under and around the canoe. Help your child decide whether the fog around the canoe and on top of the lake is water in the form of solid, liquid, or gas.

Some things float, some things sink

Do It Yourself

Have fun together experimenting to see what floats in a sink or bathtub full of water. Ask your child to guess whether each object will sink or float. Then try and see.

Imagine a big pond, or a deep puddle, or even your own bathtub, full of water.

Now imagine what happens if you put a little toy boat on top of the water. It stays on top. It floats.

What happens if you put a rock on top of the water and let go of it? Something very different happens. The rock falls down through the water. It does not float. It sinks.

Light Helps Us See

THE SUN MAKES LIGHT, and that light shines down all over the places where we live. Plants use sunlight to make food. People and other animals use sunlight to see.

In the daytime, it's bright outside. There is light all around because the sun is shining in the sky.

In the nighttime, it's dark outside. The sun cannot be seen up in the sky anymore.

Do It Yourself

Go with your child into a small closet or room with lights but no windows. Keep the light on, and ask what your child sees. Now turn the light off and ask again. People need light in order to see.

People turn on lights at night

When it's dark outside, people find other ways to make light. They light fires and candles. They turn on electric lights or even use flashlights. The light made by people is called artificial light. It helps us see things at night, when the sun goes down and there is no longer any sunlight shining around us.

New Words

"Artificial" means something that people have made, not something that comes from nature. Lightbulbs and flashlights were made in factories by people. They give us artificial light. Help your child find examples of light from nature—fire or sunlight, for instance.

Light passes through some things but not through others

When you turn on a flashlight, light travels out from it. Light can keep traveling through some things, like glass. That is why we can look through a window to see things outside, and it's why we see and feel the sunshine coming through the window.

Take a Look
Ask your child how many shadows she sees. And how many people? Help her trace the path of sunlight from bodies to shadows.

Light travels in a straight line. When it reaches a solid object, it can't curve around it. Solid objects block the light. They make shadows behind them where the light can't reach. Shadows can have the same shape as the object that blocked the light, or they can make that shape look a little different.

Air Is Invisible,
But It's Everywhere

Do It Yourself

Gently blow on your child's hand. What does he feel? He feels the air that has moved from your mouth to his hand.

YOU CAN'T SEE the air, but it is everywhere. Air is invisible, but you can still see what it does. You can see how the air moves leaves on a tree when the wind blows. You can feel the air, too. When you wave a fan in front of your face, you can't see anything touching you, but you feel the air moving across your cheek.

Air takes up space

You can't see it, but air takes up space. When you blow air into a balloon, it gets larger as you fill it up with air. When you blow bubbles, they are full of air.

Moving air makes sounds

Air also carries sound. Anything that shakes or vibrates, even just a little, shakes the air and makes a noise. In outer space, where there is no air, there is no sound.

Do It Yourself
Find other household objects that fill up with air: balloons, swimming floats, tires, inflatable toys.

Take a Look
The boy is playing a musical instrument called a tuba. He blows air into it and sound comes out. Talk through answers to these questions: Where does the air go in? Where does the sound come out?

Take a Look

Talk about this picture together. What is the wind pushing in this picture, making it move? Help your child use his finger to trace the way the wind is blowing.

Do It Yourself

Make a clothesline yourself, either outside or in the kitchen, hanging a thin fabric over a towel rack. Ask your child to be the wind and make the fabric move.

Air can push things when it moves

Air is strong enough to push things around.

Moving air sends sailboats scooting across the water. Moving air makes flags flap and wave on their flagpoles. As the air moves, it can lift a kite high up into the sky.

164

Art

■ Young children make art with great pleasure, learning as they go. To make the most of such enthusiasm, keep a variety of materials on hand at home—fingerpaints, tempera paints with brushes, colored markers, modeling clay, and so on—and arrange an area where your child can use them without concern for messes or spills.

Likewise, preschoolers can be drawn into eager appreciation of art works made by others. Here is a selection of works of art by known artists, both traditional and modern, with features that make them especially appealing to preschoolers.

Read-aloud text and parent suggestions provide ways to look at and talk about this art together. Traditional paintings—and even sculptures—often seem to tell a story. Modern art gives you a chance to talk about the basic elements of art: color, line, and shape. Continue the conversation by visiting art museums together and enjoying paintings and sculptures in person.

EDWARD HICKS

Noah's Ark

Take a Look

Look together at the animals in this painting. Help your child name them. Ask where they are going. What else can your child see in the painting? "Do you think a storm is coming soon? How do you know? What do the colors tell about the weather?"

THIS PAINTING tells the story of a man named Noah, who lived a long, long time ago. Noah heard that a big rainstorm was coming, so big it might cause a terrible flood. He made a special boat, called an ark. He invited two of every animal in the world to come live in his ark, so they would be safe and not drown in the flood. The ark kept Noah and the animals safe all through the rainstorm and the flood. When they saw a rainbow, they came out of the ark. Noah and all the animals started living on land again.

EMILE MUNIER

The New Pets

A MAN named Emile Munier [ay-MEEL MEW-nyay] decided that this moment during an ordinary day would make a good painting.

What is happening in this painting? Does it make you feel happy or sad? Can you tell me why? Does this painting make you think about a special moment in your own life?

Do these children look like people you know? They look like they lived long ago, don't they? How can you tell?

What do you think each person in this painting is saying?

What About You?

Invite your child to change this painting in his imagination so it looks more like today. "What shall we change? The clothing? Shall we give the children shoes? Where should they be sitting? What other kind of pet might they have?"

JONATHAN EASTMAN JOHNSON

The Old Stagecoach

New Words

Help your child under-
stand that people rode
in stagecoaches long
ago, before anyone
had a car. A stage-
coach had big wheels.
(This one in the paint-
ing has lost its wheels.)
A horse pulled the
stagecoach down
the road.

Do It Yourself

Point to one of the
figures in this painting.
Ask your child to make
her body look just like
that child's.

THIS IS A PAINTING that shows a lot of things happening. Let's look at one part of the picture at a time and figure it all out.

I'm going to cover all but the lefthand part of the picture. Now what do you see? A boy and a girl in old-fashioned clothes, walking somewhere. Now I'll show you a little more. What are these two boys doing? They look like they are running and kicking. What might they be pretending to be?

Now I'll show you a bit more. Do you see people wearing hats and sitting way up high on top of something? Do you know what it is? How about the next people?

Now let's look at the whole painting. What is happening? Every child is doing something in this picture. What are they doing? Does it look like they're having fun?

Domino Players

WHEN WE LOOK at this painting by a man named Horace Pippin, it's like visiting somebody else's house. Let's see what we can learn about these people by looking closely at the painting.

What room of the house are these people in? How do you know? Are the people in this picture old or young? What are they doing? Some are playing dominoes. Are they enjoying the game of dominoes? Is everybody interested in playing? Are they doing anything else?

What colors has the artist used in this painting? There are not many bright colors, are there? Most of the colors that the artist chose are neutral colors, like gray, white, black, and brown. Does that make the painting feel happy or sad?

Take a Look

There is a woman in this picture doing something quite unusual. Ask your child if he can find her—she is smoking a pipe!

What About You?

Does your child know about dominoes? Talk about this game or others that he and his friends or family play together at home.

HORACE PIPPIN

ROMARE BEARDEN

Sunday after the Sermon

Talk & Think

What does the title of this painting mean? Talk with your child about a "sermon" and where people would hear it—at church on a Sunday morning. Does that give clues on why the artist gave this painting this title?

THIS PICTURE was made by an African-American artist named Romaire Bearden. What do you recognize in it? Do you think it's a picture of people inside or outside? How can you tell?

This picture is not a painting. It is a collage [coe-LAHZH]. Mr. Bearden took pieces of paper and pasted them down, almost as if they were parts of a puzzle.

How many people are in this picture? What can you see around them? Do they look dressed up? Why do you think so?

170

The Snail

A FRENCH ARTIST named Henri Matisse [on-REE mah-TEECE] made
this work of art. It is also a collage. See the pieces of colored paper
that the artist pasted down on another piece of paper to
make his collage? What colors did he use?

Matisse called this collage "The Snail." Look at the
real snail and see why. A snail shell makes a spiral shape.
Now try to trace the spiral shape made of cut bits of paper
in this collage.

Do It Yourself
Together, trace spirals
here and in the art.

HENRI MATISSE

People and Dog in Sun

Take a Look

Help your child trace the lines that Miró drew to make this painting. Talk about how they cross and form shapes, then he colored in those shapes. Your child can make a work of art that way, too.

Talk & Think

Ask your child how old she thinks Joan Miró was when he made this painting. He was 54 years old!

THE NAME of this painting tells us that it shows people, a dog, and a sun. Do you see two people? How do you know they are people? Do you see a dog? What tells you it is a dog? Do you see the sun? Is it the same color as the sun in the sky outside?

The person who painted this painting was named Joan Miró [ZHWAN mee-RO]. Miró liked to make pictures that didn't look exactly like things do in real life. His art is called "abstract art."

Abstract art uses lines, shapes, and colors in unusual ways. It shows interesting designs or patterns instead of real things. You get new ideas and feelings by looking at abstract art.

JOAN MIRÓ

172

PAUL KLEE

Senecio

HERE IS ANOTHER example of abstract art. What does it look like to you? A face, maybe? Point to the things that might be parts of a face. Eyes? Eyebrows? Cheeks? Nose? Neck? How is this different from a face in real life?

The artist, Paul Klee [KLAY], also called this "Head of Man." It looks like he made a circle for the head, then used lines to divide it into parts. Show me the lines. What color are the parts?

New Words
Talk with your child about the part of this painting that looks like a wall behind the head, introducing the word "background." Look at other paintings to find the background in them, too.

HENRI ROUSSEAU

The Sleeping Gypsy

Take a Look

Begin this page by asking your child, "What do you think the lion is doing in this picture? And what is the man doing?"

New Words

Talk with your child about the title, "The Sleeping Gypsy," explaining that a "gypsy" is a person who travels so much, he might sleep in a new place every night.

SOMETIMES PAINTINGS tell stories. This painting is like a dream or a fairy tale. It tells a story that probably wouldn't happen in real life.

First let's talk about what we see in the picture.

Is it night or day? How can you tell? Where does it look like this is taking place? What is in the background? What else do you see in the picture?

How is the sleeping man dressed? Does he look frightened or happy? What does the man have near him? What is he holding? Let's look at the lion. Does it look mean or friendly?

Let's make up the fairy tale to go with this painting. You tell the story. "Once upon a time . . ."

174

SONIA DELAUNAY

Rhythm

THIS ARTIST, named Sonia Delaunay, made a lot of pictures like this one and called all of them "Rhythm."

What is rhythm? Let's clap rhythms together. A rhythm can be fast . . . or slow. A rhythm can be simple . . . or a rhythm can be complicated. We can clap many different rhythms. Usually people think that rhythm is made of sounds. But Sonia Delaunay thinks that rhythm can be made out of shapes and colors, too.

Take a Look

Ask your child to help you find all the circles in this painting. Then talk about the lines: "Do you see lines that curve? Do you see any lines that are straight?" Then see how many colors you can find together.

The Little Dancer

Talk & Think

Talk with your child about what the girl in the sculpture is going to do. "What kind of clothing is she wearing? Her skirt is called a tutu." Look together at her special ballet shoes. Now invite your child to stand in this same position.

Do It Yourself

You and your child will enjoy reading books about this sculpture:

Degas and the Little Dancer by L. Anholt

Marie in Fourth Position by A. Littlesugar

EDGAR DEGAS

THIS ART WORK is not a painting. It is not flat, like a drawing on paper. It is a sculpture, like something you might make out of modeling clay.

When you look at a sculpture, you can walk all around it. You can see it from the front, the back, and both sides. Can you find other sculptures in your home or in your town? They can be big or small.

This sculpture is made out of a hard metal called bronze. The artist, named Edgar Degas [day-GAH], used cloth, too. Can you find the girl's skirt and hair ribbon? They are made of real cloth.

Edgar Degas thought ballerinas were graceful and beautiful. He made many sculptures and paintings of dancers.

Blue Hippo

THIS SCULPTURE is small enough to hold in your hand. It was made a long, long time ago, so it is very old. We do not know who made it, but we do know that it was made in a country called Egypt. Egypt is part of Africa. People have taken very good care of this little blue sculpture for all the many years since it was first made.

What kind of animal is this? A hippopotamus! Here is a picture of a real hippo. Is it the same color as this little sculpture? The artist made this sculpture a different color from a live hippopotamus. Art doesn't always have to look exactly like things do in real life.

You can see this blue hippo sculpture by visiting a big art museum in New York City. An art museum is a special place where paintings, drawings, sculptures, and other works of art are kept safely so that many people can come look at them.

Take a Look
Point to the designs painted on the side of this hippo sculpture and ask your child what they look like. Some people think they are pictures of plants that grew where this hippo lived.

Do It Yourself
Use modeling clay or Play-Doh to make a sculpture of your favorite animal.

WHAT
Parents
OF PRESCHOOLERS
NEED TO KNOW

Choosing a Preschool for Your Child

THE LESSONS AND ACTIVITIES in the Core Knowledge Home Preschool Program derive from the curriculum of the Core Knowledge Preschools. Parents using these books at home can be sure that they are giving their three- to five-year-olds solid learning with sequence, methods, and content developed through research and practice.

A home is not a school, though, and some essential elements of early childhood learning might be missing with a home-based preschool experience as compared with the social milieu of other like-aged children in a school setting. For that reason, we offer advice to parents in the process of choosing a preschool for their children.

A good preschool will teach your child many important concepts and skills. The experience will lay down an essential foundation for all future learning. Children attending preschool learn how to interact with others their age, how to use materials, and how to behave in a school setting. Every one of these elements contributes to school success in the years to come.

Unfortunately, however, preschool programs vary in quality. Some are very good, many are mediocre, and others are downright detrimental in the effect they have on children's development.

Before selecting a preschool, parents should talk to parents and others in the community. Kindergarten teachers at your local elementary school can be a good source of information. Ask them which preschools consistently send well-prepared students to kindergarten. Parents should visit preschool programs themselves, to observe, take in the atmosphere, and make their own decisions about what's best for their child.

The following pages offer questions to keep in mind as you are choosing a preschool.

STAFF

How long have current staff members been teaching at this school? Did any staff members leave during the past year?

What happens when a teacher is absent?

What are the professional qualifications of each staff member? Do teachers have college degrees and, if not, what other kind of training do they have? What did this training cover and how many hours did it entail?

How many adults are in the classroom, working with the children at all times? For three- to four-year-olds, class size should not exceed more than 16 to 18 children with two adults.

What are the qualifications of the program administrator or director? How long has he/she supervised this school?

PHYSICAL ENVIRONMENT

Is the furniture and equipment child-size?

Are the following kinds of materials readily available:

- picture books for children to read? story books and information books?
- writing materials: paper, markers, pencils, alphabet stamps, magnetic letters, etc.?
- art supplies: easels, paint, clay, child-size scissors, construction paper, etc.?
- pretend play materials: dolls, dress-up clothes, and other props?
- blocks: wooden blocks of various shapes, large cardboard or plastic blocks?
- puzzles? simple board games?
- small manipulative materials: Legos and other construction toys, pegs and pegboards, large wooden beads and lacing strings, etc.?
- outdoor play materials: balls, riding toys, sand toys, slides, swings, climbing equipment, etc.?

Are there sufficient educational materials and toys for the number of children in the program and are all materials in good repair?

Are there displays of the children's writing and artwork in the room? Are there displays of group writing experiences that the children have completed with the teacher, such as descriptions of things that they have done together?

SOCIAL AND EMOTIONAL ENVIRONMENT

How do teachers interact with children? Do they respond promptly to children? Do they express nurturing behaviors in tone of voice, facial expression, eye contact, and physical affection? Do they appear to enjoy working with young children, or do they appear frustrated and overworked?

Do teachers actively help children learn how to interact and play with other children?

How do teachers deal with unacceptable behavior, such as hitting, pushing, or biting?

PROGRAM AND ACTIVITIES

Is there a posted schedule of activities with a predictable routine each day?

Are there times for the following kinds of activities each day: large group instruction with the whole class; small group instruction (4 to 6 children at a time); play time, with the area and toys for play selected by the child?

Are books read aloud every day, both to the whole group and small groups of children?

Is there a written curriculum identifying what children are expected to learn?

Do the teachers prepare written lesson plans for the different group instructional activities each day?

Does a day include a variety of activities in the following areas:

☐ *movement and coordination:* running, hopping, jumping, throwing, catching, riding a tricycle, etc.?

☐ *literacy:* playing with the sounds of language in nursery rhymes, identifying letter names and sounds, writing letters, dictating thoughts and ideas, etc.?

☐ *math:* counting objects, identifying and writing numerals, recognizing shapes and colors, comparing objects or groups of objects, classifying, measuring, creating patterns, etc.?

☐ *science:* observing and recording observations, learning about plants, animals (including people), life cycles, and physical properties of the Earth, such as air, water, and light, etc.?

☐ *art:* exploring various media such as painting, drawing, modeling clay; looking at and talking about real works of art, etc.?

☐ *music:* singing and playing musical games, listening to various types of music, including classical music?

Do teachers model good language for children throughout the day, talking about all that is happening in the classroom, introducing new vocabulary words and concepts, and using good grammar?

Do teachers provide parents with information regarding their child's learning progress, either in parent conferences or in written reports?

SAFETY, HEALTH, AND CLEANLINESS

Is the school licensed by the state and does it meet all local safety regulations?

If food is served as part of the program, does the program comply with established food safety standards?

Have any violations of the state licensing code and/or health regulations ever been noted? What steps were taken to remedy these deficiencies?

Have there ever been any accidents at the school requiring emergency medical treatment? If so, what and how was the situation handled?

Is there at least one staff member who is certified in general first aid and CPR?

Is Your Child Ready for Kindergarten?

LEARNING EXPERIENCES during the preschool years lay the foundation for all future academic success. Whether you decide that your child should spend these important years at home or in an organized early childhood program, you will still want to do all you can to be sure she or he is ready and able to take full advantage of all that is offered come the kindergarten year.

Kindergarten-readiness does not just happen. While learning seems to come naturally, young children do not automatically acquire all the knowledge and skills they need for a positive kindergarten experience. The readiness to learn that each child brings into the kindergarten classroom comes directly from the experiences she or he has had—or has not had—in the years before.

In the past, faced with young children who were not yet ready for kindergarten, public schools sometimes suggested that parents wait another year before enrolling them. Such an approach often resulted in more harm than good, though, if the child did not spend that additional year in valuable learning experiences. In other words, simply providing more time for a child to grow up is no guarantee that she or he will be more ready for kindergarten. The key is for parents to become knowledgeable and to be constantly proactive, working together with their children and making learning a joyful and productive part of everyday life from the preschool years on.

On the next two pages, you will find a checklist of the basic knowledge and skills that all young children need for a strong start in kindergarten and elementary school. The Core Knowledge Home Preschool Program, designed around these guidelines, provides these essential learning experiences to your preschooler.

HEALTH AND PHYSICAL WELL-BEING

Go up and down steps, hop, run, jump, and climb simple equipment without losing balance.

Play catch with an adult using a beanbag or ball.

Ride a tricycle.

Maintain momentum on a swing by pumping legs.

WORK HABITS

Listen attentively to a book being read aloud to a group of children for at least 10 minutes.

Listen attentively to a book being read aloud while sitting on an adult's lap for at least 15 to 20 minutes.

Play with a toy and/or complete an age-appropriate activity during a sustained period of time, at least 15 minutes, with minimal supervision.

Follow multi-step directions.

SOCIAL AND EMOTIONAL DEVELOPMENT

Care for personal needs, such as using the bathroom independently, dressing oneself, using appropriate table manners, etc.

Recognize and greet familiar people by name.

Use verbal forms of politeness, such as "please," "thank you," "you're welcome," etc.

Follow rules established for specific settings (public places like a bookstore or church, for example).

Follow the rules of simple games.

Play cooperatively with other children, taking turns and sharing toys as necessary.

LANGUAGE

Give and respond to full name.

Clearly communicate needs, desires, and feelings.

Speak in sentences that are, for the most part, grammatically correct.

Carry on a simple conversation with an adult, taking turns, staying on topic, contributing to the conversation by answering and asking questions, etc.

Sequentially describe a personal experience.

Ask and answer questions.

Understand and use words pertaining to position in space, such as "under/over," "in/on," "up/down," etc.

Understand and use words pertaining to time, such as the names of the days of the week, "morning/afternoon/evening," "today/tomorrow/yesterday," etc.

LITERACY

Recite familiar nursery rhymes from memory.

Identify rhyming words in familiar nursery rhymes.

Give the beginning sound heard in a spoken word.

Answer questions about what is happening in a book that is being read aloud.

Retell a familiar story in child's own words.

Pretend to read a book, pointing out the words on a page, where to start reading and in what direction, turning the pages correctly, etc.

Name the letters and give the sounds of the letters in his or her first name.

Draw and copy simple lines and marks.

Write first name, even if some mistakes are present.

Cut straight lines with scissors.

Dictate thoughts and ideas to an adult.

MATH

Identify whether objects are the same or different.

Complete puzzles with 8 to 15 pieces.

Rote-count from 1 to 10.

Count up to 6 objects correctly.

Compare groups of objects, using words like "more," "less," "equal," and "the same."

Compare the size of objects, using words like "large/small," "long/short," "thick/thin," etc.

Categorize objects according to a single characteristic, such as color, shape, or size.

Continue a pattern of objects.

Identify some numerals.

GENERAL KNOWLEDGE

Recognize and name:

- parts of the body
- colors and shapes
- household items
- food and clothing
- animals and their habitats, such as farm, ocean, jungle, desert

Identify and explain the use of the five senses and the associated body parts.

Identify the body parts of a particular animal, its needs, and its life cycle.

Identify the parts of a plant, its needs, and its life cycle.

Talk about some properties of water, light, and air.

Reading Aloud with Your Child

READING ALOUD with your preschooler can be a pleasure for you both. Start by getting comfortable. Cuddle up, with your child on your lap or next to you, plenty close so she can see and touch the pages of the book, too. Have fun—drop your inhibitions—act out the book as you read it. Use different voices for different characters, express yourself with voice, face, and gestures. Make the story come alive.

It's best to start with shorter readings for a younger child. Nursery rhymes, poems, fingerplays, and simple stories are all good choices. Plan on reading for five to ten minutes, but pay attention to your child's interest level and body language. If he starts to squirm, it's probably time to stop. Read again later in the day, or tomorrow.

A child actually gains experience as a listener, sitting and listening for longer periods of time over the months and years of your reading aloud together. A child ready to go to kindergarten will be able to listen to picture books for up to thirty minutes. Some might even be ready to listen to simple chapter books by then. (See our list of Great Books for Preschoolers in the Resources section, coming up.)

Reading aloud together should be fun and educational at the same time. Here are some pointers on how to make the most of the time you spend reading with your child. The first time you share a new story, simply read it all the way through, with relatively few interruptions. Read clearly and slowly, but at a normal pace. If your child looks puzzled or asks a question, of course you should pause in the story and talk things over as you can.

As adults, we sometimes think that hearing the same story is boring. Not so for young children! They love hearing the same stories over and over, and they discover something new and interesting every time. Here's a plan: just remember STORY!

START WITH TITLE AND PICTURES ●

First look at the book's cover or illustrated title page together. Read the title out loud, pointing to each word as you read it. Talk about what the title might mean, using pictures nearby for clues. Name the author and illustrator, if they are identified, so your child learns that real people make books.

Focus next on the pictures. Help your child name and describe what she sees. Then, before starting to read, ask her what she thinks the story will be about. The point is not to tell the story accurately, but rather to find picture clues about character, theme, location, or plot. Hers may differ from the actual story, but that's okay!

TELL THE STORY ●

Read aloud, one or two pages at a time. Read the words clearly and expressively. At first, point to each word as you read. Granted, it would be tedious to do this throughout the entire story, but start by doing it on the first page or so.

Read with animation. Use different voices for different characters. For example, when you read "Goldilocks and the Three Bears," use a loud, assertive voice for Papa Bear, a quieter voice for Mama Bear, and a teeny-tiny squeak for Baby Bear.

OFFER INFORMATION ●

At the end of every page or two, pause and look at the illustrations together. Talk about them with your child. Ask what he sees. Use this conversation to confirm and clarify the words you have just read.

Look out for words or phrases that your child might not understand. Feel free to pause as you read and explain, rephrase, or give examples. We have identified a few words in these anthology readings that might be new to a preschooler, but you know your child best and may notice other words that need some explaining. An ever-growing vocabulary is a rich reward for a child whose parent reads aloud.

When you are offering information, you are doing the essential task of building your child's vocabulary. The importance of helping develop a rich oral vocabulary during the preschool years cannot be overstated. Reading stories and nonfiction books aloud is one of the surest ways. Every time your child listens to a book or story, he will be exposed to words that often are not part of everyday spoken language.

Unlike many contemporary children's books, the selections in this anthology have been expressly written to include words that are challenging and evocative, designed to paint vivid pictures in the reader's and listener's minds. The parent notes in this anthology highlight a few such words, giving suggestions as to how to explain them to your child. Once you have talked about these words in the context of the story, make an effort to incorporate them into everyday conversations with your child, as the occasion arises.

For example, the parent notes in the story of "The City Mouse and the Country Mouse" suggest that you explain the word "feast" as meaning a large meal associated with a special occasion. After reading this story, you might make a conscious effort to use the word "feast" soon with your child: "I'll bet that we will have a real feast when we go to Grandma's house for dinner this Sunday! I'll bet we'll eat in her fancy dining room, and we'll have lots of your favorite foods." It is only in hearing you use these new words in repeated, familiar contexts that your child will really begin to make sense of them. And as he hears them often, he will begin to use them comfortably and appropriately himself, in his own growing vocabulary.

A word of caution, though. While each anthology selection has a lot of colorful and interesting language likely to be unfamiliar to your preschooler at the start, it is important not to bombard her with explanations for lots of new words in a single sitting. Don't try to discuss more than three or four new words per read-aloud session. Remember that young children like to hear the same story read over and over, and so each reading of a story with rich vocabulary represents another opportunity to talk about the new and interesting words it contains.

There are many ways to explain new words to your preschooler as you come upon them during read-aloud time. Do all you can to keep your explanation at a level that your child can understand. Wordy, dictionary-like definitions—definitions that use more difficult words to explain the one in question—will not work. Instead, try simple, careful paraphrasing. Read the sentence from the story that contains a new word, and then repeat the very same sentence, this time substituting a synonymous word or phrase that your child already knows.

For example, at the beginning of "The City Mouse and Country Mouse," one sentence says, "The other mouse lived in a large, stylish house in the city." Perhaps you have a hunch that your child is not familiar with the word "stylish." Read this sentence one more time slowly, pausing on the word. After the second reading, you might say "That means that the other mouse lived in a big, fancy house in the city that was the latest thing. It was a really cool house. Stylish means fancy, the latest thing, something that is so cool, everybody wants it."

To further illustrate the meaning of a word unfamiliar to your preschooler, you can also point to the pictures alongside the story. In the case of the City Mouse's house, for example, you could point to the city houses, shown in the distance in the first illustration, and say, "The houses in the city were big and had lots of windows. A house with lots of windows was very stylish. Everybody wanted a house with lots of windows."

Another way to help your child understand a new word is to relate it to something within your child's own experience. "The City Mouse's house was stylish," you can say. "These jeans that you are wearing, with the colorful embroidery on them, are really stylish, too. They are very fancy and just the latest thing. I think they are cool—don't you? They are such stylish jeans." By relating the word to your child's own experience, you help her see how to use it in her own world and in her own vocabulary.

Using any or every one of these tactics to introduce new words to your child, you will be taking advantage of each read-aloud to help your child discover the richness of our language. Introducing new vocabulary is one of the most important things you do as you read together with your child, whether you are reading the stories and the nonfiction selections of this anthology or reading other books, stories, and magazines. Always keep your eyes and ears attuned for new words—words that deserve an extra few minutes to be introduced deliberately to your child, then used consciously during the course of your day today, so that those words come to form part of your child's working vocabulary.

We strongly recommend that before you read any selection aloud with your child, you take the time to read it to yourself. Do all that you can to read the passage through the eyes of a preschooler. Make a mental note of the words that may be unknown to your child, and pick out a few to explain when you sit down together to share the story.

In this way, these anthology selections will never get old. They will grow with your child as you share them again and again throughout her preschool years.

REVIEW AND DISCUSS ·

At the end of each page or two as well, pause to make sure your child understands not only the vocabulary that has been part of the story but also the plot itself. Ask a question about a character or about something that has just happened.

As you read together more, your child will become more skillful at listening and answering simple questions. Then you can ask questions that require him to go beyond recalling immediate details. Parent notes alongside the stories in this anthology suggest such questions, but your own child's experience and interests will bring up other possibilities as well.

YOUR CHILD'S TURN!

During or after a story, asking questions is a good way to help your child understand. Here are a few ones that work well:

"Have you ever…(*done what one of the characters in the story is doing*)?"

"Have you ever felt…(*an emotion felt by a character in the story*)? When?"

"What do you think might happen next?"

"Why … (*did something happen, does a character feel a certain way, etc.*)?"

"How do you think the story will end?"

After you finish the story, ask your child to tell it to you. (If her attention is flagging, postpone this request to another read-aloud time.) At first, retelling the story might be hard. There are good ways to help her. Move through the book, looking at each illustration, and ask her to tell you what is happening as a way to retell the story. Her early attempts may be disjointed, but that's all right.

You can also ask key questions about each illustration, then restate what he tells you in complete sentences. Use standard phrases and story connectors, like "Once upon a time," "First," "Next," "Then," and "The End." Soon he will be using those, too.

READING NONFICTION?

Nonfiction read-alouds are just as important as stories. From them, your child can learn about all sorts of fascinating subjects. In this anthology, we include selections in history, science, and art. The five-step STORY approach can be more difficult to use when reading nonfiction, which is dense in vocabulary and information. Read only a couple of nonfiction pages at a time, spend lots of time talking about the illustrations, and find ways to relate the contents to your child's own experience.

THE PLEASURES OF READING ALOUD

The hours you spend reading aloud with your preschooler are precious—not only for your child, as a learning experience and as a time to feel close and comfortable with a caring adult, but also for you, as the person who is helping to nurture this child in so many important and wonderful ways. You will look back with pride and satisfaction, remembering these times and knowing that your child's engagement in learning began during the time you spent reading aloud.

Enjoying Music
with Your Preschooler

MUSIC BECKONS IRRESISTIBLY to young children. Watch preschoolers' faces and bodies when they hear rhythm and sound—they light up and move, eagerly and enthusiastically. They communicate comfortably, express themselves creatively, let out all sorts of thoughts and emotions as they interact with music. In a word, young children think music is a lot of fun, so do all you can to make the most of the situation. Lose your own inhibitions, forget all concerns about whether you are musically inclined or whether you can sing or play an instrument. Those things don't matter when you are enjoying music with your child. Follow his lead, and have fun too! Sing songs together, listen to different kinds of music, move, dance and enjoy.

The experience of music actually offers important learning opportunities. Careful listening helps fine-tune your child's aural skills, so he becomes more adept at paying attention to sounds and auditory details. Including musical experiences into your child's day helps build a set of important skills: hearing whether sounds are the same or different, learning to associate a sound with its source, learning to identify what instrument makes which sound, and so on. These skills become the foundation on which children build in later years when they are asked to tune their ears to hear how certain letters sound and to associate those sounds with written letters. In other words, listening to music builds skills that help a child become a better reader.

Even more fundamentally, some studies now suggest, early musical experiences may enhance the development of certain cognitive skills, such as recognition and recall of spatial relationships—the skills it takes, for example, to put together a puzzle. Other math-related skills may also be promoted by introducing a variety of musical experiences early in a child's life. By clapping or counting out rhythms along with a familiar song, for example, your child is interacting deeply with structures shared among music, math, and the world of ideas.

There are so many ways to include music in your child's day, and so many different kinds of music to share with her. In this anthology, we have offered the lyrics of a number of tried and true children's songs, with suggestions on ways to connect movement and fingerplay along with singing. The more you sing these songs, the more familiar they become—a process that endears a song to children and makes it all the more fun to sing together, over and over. Find other creative ways to play with songs as you sing them. You can make homemade rhythm instruments with pots and pans, wooden spoons or metal kitchen utensils; you can make homemade rattles by filling tight-lidded plastic containers with uncooked rice, dried beans, or buttons.

Your child will enjoy moving to recorded music, too, whether it's folk songs or orchestral symphonies. A flowing colored scarf or crepe paper streamers can make the dance seem even more fun and fantastic. Dances to music can be freeform or patterned. You can suggest that she try different movements, like skipping or hopping, swaying or bending, depending on the rhythm that she hears. Ask what the music sounds like—a lullaby for a baby? a marching parade? a bird flying in the sky?—then encourage your child to act out those ideas in time with the music. As your child becomes more familiar with recorded instrumental music, you can even begin to help her identify the instruments: the high-pitched piccolo, the breathy flute, the vibrato violin, the oompah tuba.

Music can be a pleasure to share; singing or listening to a recording can be a relaxing way to spend time together. Below, we list the pieces of music that teachers enjoy using in Core Knowledge Preschools. The collection is available on a single CD, produced by Core Knowledge and included on the list of Great Music that follows.

Preschoolers love these works of music:

Georges Bizet, Overture to *Carmen*
Johannes Brahms, "Cradle Song" (also called "Brahms's Lullaby)
Claude Debussy, "Cakewalk" from *Children's Corner Suite*
Victor Herbert, "March of the Toys" from *Babes in Toyland*
Aram Khachaturian, "Sabre Dance" from *Gayane*
Wolfgang Amadeus Mozart, Variations on "Ah, vous dirai-je maman!"
Jacques Offenbach, "Can-Can" from *Gaîté parisienne*
Amilcare Ponchielli, "Dance of the Hours"
Robert Schumann, "Dreams" from *Scenes from Childhood*
Johann Strauss, Jr., "Donner und Blitz [Thunder and Lightning]" waltz
Peter Ilich Tchaikovsky, *The Nutcracker Suite*
Heitor Villa-Lobos, "The Little Train of the Caipira"

Resources

Parents who want to explore the Core Knowledge Preschool Program further and those interested in purchasing materials prepared specifically for Core Knowledge Preschools—are invited to visit our website: www.coreknowledge.org.

Below we list books and music that will bring joy and learning to preschoolers.

Great Books for Preschoolers

STORIES

Aardema, Verna.
  Borreguita and the Coyote

Albert, Richard. *Alejandro's Gift*

Axtell, David.
  We're Going on a Lion Hunt

Belemans, Ludwig. *Madeleine*

Bernier-Grand, Carmen T. **Juan Bobo:**
  Four Folk Tales from Puerto Rico

Brown, Margaret Wise. *Goodnight Moon*

Brown, Margaret Wise.
  The Runaway Bunny

Burton, Virginia Lee. *Mike Mulligan
  and the Steam Shovel*

Carle, Eric. *Does a Kangaroo Have
  a Mother Too?*

Carle, Eric. *The Tiny Seed*

Carle, Eric. *The Very Hungry Caterpillar*

Cohn, Amy, ed. *From Sea to Shining
  Sea: A Treasury of American Folklore*

Cooney, Barbara. *Emma*

Cooney, Barbara. *Miss Rumphius*

Crews, Donald. *Bigmama's*

Crews, Donald. *Freight Train*

Day, Alexandra. *Good Dog, Carl*

DePaola, Tomie. *Strega Nona*

Eastman, P. D. *Are You My Mother?*

Eastman, P. D. *Go, Dog, Go*

Flack, Marjorie. *Ask Mr. Bear*

Freeman, Don. *Corduroy*

Ga'g, Wanda. *Millions of Cats*

Gonzalez, Lucia M. *The Bossy Gallito*

Herman, Gail. *The Lion and the Mouse*

Hoberman, Mary Ann.
  A House Is a House for Me

Hoberman, Mary Ann.
  I Know an Old Lady

Hoffman, Mary. *Amazing Grace*

Isaacs, Anne E. *Swamp Angel*

Johnson, Crockett.
  Harold and the Purple Crayon

Johnston, Tony.
  The Tale of Rabbit and Coyote

Keats, Ezra Jack. *The Snowy Day*

Krauss, Ruth. *The Carrot Seed*

Lamorisse, Albert. *The Red Balloon*

Leaf, Munroe. *Ferdinand*

Lester, Julius. *Sam and the Tigers*

Lin, Grace. *Kite Flying*

Lionni, Leo. *Frederick*

Lionni, Leo. *Swimmy*

Martin Jr., Bill. *Brown Bear, Brown Bear, What Do You See?*

Mayer, Mercer. *A Boy, a Dog and a Frog*

McCloskey, Robert. *Blueberries for Sal*

McCloskey, Robert. *Make Way for Ducklings*

Mitchell, Margaree King. *Uncle Jed's Barbershop*

Mosel, Arlene. *Tikki Tikki Tembo*

Peterson, John. *The Littles*

Piper, Watty. *The Little Engine That Could*

Rathmann, Peggy. *Good Night, Gorilla*

Ray, H. A. *Curious George*

Rosenberry, Vera. *Who Is in the Garden?*

Scieszka, Jon. *The True Story of the 3 Little Pigs*

Sendak, Maurice. *Where the Wild Things Are*

Slobodkina, Esphyr. *Caps for Sale*

Steptoe, John. *Mufaro's Beautiful Daughters*

Stiles Gannett, Ruth. *My Father's Dragon*

Seuss, Dr. *The Cat in the Hat*

Takeshita, Fumiko. *The Park Bench*

Trivizas, Eugene. *The Three Little Wolves and the Big Bad Pig*

Thong, Roseanne. *Round Is a Mooncake*

Torres, Leyla. *The Kite Festival*

Wood, Audrey. *Quick as a Cricket*

RHYMES, FINGERPLAYS, AND POEMS

Beal, Pamela Conn. *Wee Sing Children's Songs and Fingerplays*

Ciardi, John. *Doodle Soup*

Field, Eugene. *Wynken, Blynken, & Nod*

Frost, Robert. *Stopping by Woods on a Snowy Evening*

Frost, Robert. *A Swinger of Birches: Poems of Robert Frost for Young People*

Kennedy, X. J., et al. *Talking Like the Rain: A Read to Me Book of Poems*

Hall, Donald. *The Oxford Illustrated Book of American Children's Poems*

Lear, Edward. *The Owl and the Pussycat Board Book*

Prelutsky, Jack. *It's Raining Pigs and Noodles*

Prelutsky, Jack. *The New Kid on the Block*

Prelutsky, Jack. *Ride a Purple Pelican*

Silverstein, Shel. *Runny Babbit: A Billy Sook*

Sing a Song of Popcorn: Every Child's Book of Poems

Stevenson, Robert Louis. *A Child's Garden of Verses*

HISTORY

Borden, Louise W. *A. Lincoln and Me*

Fritz, Jean. *Can't You Make Them Behave, King George?*

George, Jean Craighead. *The First Thanksgiving*

Herman, John. *Red, White, and Blue*

Kellogg, Steven. *Yankee Doodle*

Kindersley, Anabel. *Children Just Like Me*

Kay, Verla. *Tattered Sails*

Krauss Melmed, Laura. *The First Thanksgiving Day: A Counting Story*

Lems-Tardif, Gina. *Pilgrim Children Had Many Chores*

A Life Like Mine: How Children Live Around the World

Mara, Wil. *Martin Luther King, Jr.*

Martin Jr., Bill. *I Pledge Allegiance*

Marzollo, Jean. *Happy Birthday, Martin Luther King*

McGovern, Ann. *The Pilgrims' First Thanksgiving*

Moore, Johnny Ray. *The Story of Martin Luther King, Jr*

Pingry, Patricia A. *The Story of Abraham Lincoln*

Pingry, Patricia A. *The Story of America's Birthday*

Pingry, Patricia A. *The Story of George Washington*

Skarmeas, Nancy J. *The Story of Thanksgiving*

Spier, Peter. *People*

Wallner, Alexandra. *Betsy Ross*

Winters, Kay. *Abe Lincoln: The Boy Who Loved Books*

SCIENCE

Allen, Judy. *Are You an Ant?*

Allen, Judy. *Are You a Butterfly?*

Allen, Judy. *Are You a Ladybug?*

Aliki. *My Five Senses*

Asch, Frank. *Water*

Branley, Franklyn. *Air Is All Around You*

Brenner, Barbara. *Thinking About Ants*

Davies, Nicola. *Deserts*

Davies, Nicola. *Oceans and Seas*

Dorros, Arthur. *Feel the Wind*

First Animal Encyclopedia

Fleming, Denise. *Time to Sleep*

Fredericks, Anthony D. *Under One Rock: Bugs, Slugs and Other Ughs*

Grossman, Patricia. *Very First Things to Know About Ants*

Guiberson, Brenda Z. *Cactus Hotel*

Heiligman, Deborah. *From Caterpillar to Butterfly*

Heller, Ruth. *The Reason for a Flower*

Hewitt, Sally. *Animal Homes*

Hickman, Pamela. *A New Butterfly*

Hickman, Pamela. *A New Frog*

Jordan, Helene. *How a Seed Grows*

Kalman, Bobbie. *How a Plant Grows*

Kimiko, Kajikawa. *Sweet Dreams: How Animals Sleep*

Lanczak Williams, Rozanne. *Whose Forest Is It?*

Lester, Alison. *Imagine*

Marzollo, Jean. *I'm a Seed*

Morris, Neil. *Deserts*

Morris, Neil. *Oceans*

Muther, Connie. *A Monarch Journal*

My First Animal Board Book

My First Farm Book

Nicholson, Sue.
  A Day at Greenhill Farm

Pfeffer, Wendy. *A Log's Life*

Pledger, Maurice. *By the Seashore*

Pledger, Maurice. *In the Forest*

Pledger, Maurice. *In the Ocean*

Provensen, Alice and Martin. *Our Animal Friends at Maple Hill Farm*

Rice, David L. *Lifetimes*

Schaefer, Lola M. *This Is the Sunflower*

Simon, Seymour.
  Let's Try It Out in the Air

Simon, Seymour. *Let's Try It Out in the Water*

Swinburne, Stephen.
  Guess Whose Shadow

Touch and Feel: Wild Animals

Trapani, Iza. *What Am I? An Animal Guessing Game*

Wallace, Karen. *A Day at Seagull Beach*

Wallace, Karen. *Tale of a Tadpole*

Weidner, Kathleen. *What's Alive?*

Young, Caroline.
  The Great Animal Search

ART

Anholt, Laurence.
  Degas and the Little Dancer

Anholt, Laurence.
  Camille and the Sunflowers

Anholt, Laurence.
  Leonardo and the Flying Boy

Anholt, Laurence. *The Magical Garden of Claude Monet*

Anholt, Laurence. *Picasso and the Girl with the Pony Tail*

Lach, William. *Baby Loves*

Littlesugar, Amy.
  Marie in Fourth Position

Merberg, Julie.
  In the Garden with Van Gogh

Merberg, Julie.
  A Magical Day with Matisse

Merberg, Julie. *Dancing with Degas*

Merberg, Julie. *Sharing with Renoir*

Merberg, Julie. *Sunday with Seurat*

Micklethwait, Lucy.
  A Child's Book of Art

Micklethwait, Lucy.
  Colors: A First Art Book

Micklethwait, Lucy. *I Spy: Shapes in Art*

Micklethwait, Lucy.
  I Spy Two Eyes: Numbers in Art

Schulte, Jessica. *Can You Find It Inside?*

Schulte, Jessica.
  Can You Find It Outside?

Vincent's Colors

Weitzman, Jacqueline. *You Can't Take a Balloon into the Metropolitan Museum*

ABC AND NUMBER BOOKS

The Alphabet Book

Anno, Mitsumasa.
    Anno's Counting Book

Barrett, Judi.
    I Know Two Who Said Moo

Boynton, Sandra. *A to Z*

Calmenson, Stephanie.
    It Begins with an A

Dr. Seuss's ABC Book

Ehlert, Lois. *Eating the Alphabet:
    Fruits and Vegetables from A to Z*

Gerth, Melanie. *Ten Little Ladybugs*

Jay, Alison. *ABC: A Child's First
    Alphabet Book*

Johnson, Stephen. *Alphabet City*

Martin, Bill, and J. Archambault.
    Chicka Chicka Boom Boom

Micklethwait, Lucy.
    I Spy: An Alphabet in Art

McPhail, David. *Animals A to Z*

My First ABC Board Book

Rey, H. A
    Curious George Learns the Alphabet

Ruschak, Lynette.
    Nature by the Numbers

Schwartz, David M.
    How Much Is a Million?

Wood, Jakki. *Animal Parade*

Great Music for Preschoolers

CLASSICAL MUSIC

Best of Classical Kids Series (six CDs,
    available separately or as a set):
    Best of Bach, Beethoven, Handel,
    Mozart, Tchaikovsky, Vivaldi.
    Music for Little People

*Carnival of the Animals: Classical
    Music for Children.* Metropolitan
    Museum of Art

*Children's Classics: Peter and the Wolf;
    Carnival of the Animals; Young
    Person's Guide to the Orchestra.* Sony

*Classical Music for Children:
    A Toddler's Introduction*

*The Core Knowledge Music Collection:
    Preschool and Kindergarten.*
    Core Knowledge Foundation

*Richard Perlmutter, Beethoven's Wig:
    Sing Along Symphonies.* Rounder

NURSERY RHYMES AND OLD FAVORITES

Burl Ives Sings. Sony Wonder.

Dreamland. Putumayo Kids Series.

Hap Palmer, *Early Childhood Classics:
    Old Favorites with a New Twist.*
    Hap-Pal Music

Hap Palmer, *So Big: Activity Songs for
    Little Ones.* Hap-Pal Music

Raffi, *Singable Songs Collection.*
    Rounder

Pete Seeger, *Birds, Beasts, Bugs & Fishes Little & Big.* Smithsonian Folkways

Storytime Favorites. Music for Little People

Toddlers Sing Storytime. Music for Little People

A Treasury of Children's Songs, vols. I and II. Metropolitan Museum of Art

JAZZ, FOLK, AND WORLD MUSIC

Baby Loves Jazz. Metropolitan Museum of Art

A Child's Celebration of Folk Music. Music for Little People

A Child's Celebration of Song. Music for Little People

David Grisman & Jerry Garcia, *Not for Kids Only.* Acoustic Disc.

Jazz for Kids. Verve

Nickel Creek Band, *Little Cowpoke.* Music for Little People

ABOUT THE
Core Knowledge Foundation

THE CORE KNOWLEDGE FOUNDATION is a nonprofit, nonpartisan organization established in 1986 by E. D. Hirsch, Jr., a professor at the University of Virginia and the author of many books, including the bestseller, *Cultural Literacy*, as well as *The Schools We Need* and *The Knowledge Deficit*. For the past twenty years, the Foundation has worked to translate the ideas of Dr. Hirsch into instructional materials that make a content-rich curriculum available to children in the early grades and contribute to creating a fairer and more literate society.

The Core Knowledge movement is an educational reform based on the premise that a grade-by-grade core of common learning is necessary to ensure a sound and fair elementary education. Dr. Hirsch has argued that, for the sake of academic excellence, greater fairness, and higher literacy, early schooling should follow a solid, specific, shared core curriculum so that children establish strong foundations of knowledge. After wide consultation, the content of this core curriculum has been outlined in two books, the *Core Knowledge Preschool Sequence* and the *Core Knowledge Sequence, K–8,* which state explicitly what students should learn at each grade level. Currently, hundreds of schools and thousands of dedicated educators are participating in this school reform movement throughout the United States.

The Core Knowledge Series, of which this book is a part, is based on the same curriculum taught in Core Knowledge schools throughout the country. For more information about the Core Knowledge Foundation and Core Knowledge schools, please visit the Foundation website at www.coreknowledge.org. At our website, you will find an online bookstore, lesson plans, and additional resources and materials for parents and teachers.

About the Authors

E. D. Hirsch, Jr., is an emeritus professor at the University of Virginia and the author of *The Knowledge Deficit, The Schools We Need*, and the bestselling *Cultural Literacy* and *The Dictionary of Cultural Literacy.* He and his wife, Polly, live in Charlottesville, Virginia, where they raised their three children.

Linda Bevilacqua is the president of the Core Knowledge Foundation and was responsible for the development of the Core Knowledge preschool program that is now being used in over 1,200 preschool classrooms across the country. She and her husband, Jean-Jacques, live in Charlottesville, Virginia.

ABOUT THE ILLUSTRATORS

AMY WUMMER has been working in the field of illustration since the early 1990s. Specializing in whimsical, lighthearted themes, she is known primarily as a children's book illustrator, with over 40 titles to her credit. Amy works in pencil and ink with watercolor dyes. She and her husband, Mark, also an artist, and their three children, Jesse, Maisie, and Adam, live in Reading, Pennsylvania.

LINA CHESAK LIBERACE has been illustrating since 1988. Her images are used by editorial and corporate clients as well as in children's literature. She lives with her husband, artist Robert Liberace, and two young daughters, Celia and Ava, in Vienna, Virginia. Her work can be seen at www.linaliberace.com.

G. B. McINTOSH's illustrations have been published in both adult and children's books, including *Gather Ye Wild Things*, *Wildflowers on the Windowsill*, and *Nature By the Numbers*, a pop-up book. She and her husband, Michael Osteen, an architect, live in Charlottesville, Virginia. They have one daughter, Maisie, who attends Hofstra University.

BARBARA LEONARD GIBSON has worked as an award-winning freelance artist in the Washington-Baltimore area for 30 years. She has illustrated more than three dozen books, published by organizations including the National Geographic Society and Colonial Williamsburg and written by authors including Patricia Cornwell, Audrey Penn, and Marie and Roland Smith.

CREDITS

Editor-in-Chief of the Core Knowledge Series: E. D. Hirsch, Jr.
Author and Executive Editor: Linda Bevilacqua
Managing Editor: Susan Tyler Hitchcock
Art Director/Designer: Dorrit Green, greenink.design
Illustrators: Barbara L. Gibson (*Science*), Lina Chesak-Liberace (*Songs*),
  G. B. McIntosh (*Stories, History*), Amy Wummer (*Poems*)
Science Writer: Patricia Daniels
Science Consultant: Sally Guarino
Researchers: Janet Dustin, Judy Ladendorf of The Permissions Group, Jeanne Nicholson Siler

THIS PROJECT BENEFITED FROM GENEROUS CONTRIBUTIONS FROM THE CHALLENGE FOUNDATION AND THE WALTON FAMILY FOUNDATION.

POETRY CREDITS AND SOURCES

"Raindrops" from OUT IN THE DARK AND DAYLIGHT by Aileen Fisher. Copyright © 1980 by Aileen Fisher. By permission of Marian Reiner on behalf of the Boulder Public Library Foundation, Inc.

"Jack-o-Lantern" from RUNNY DAYS, SUNNY DAYS by Aileen Fisher. Copyright © 1958, 1986 Aileen Fisher. By permission of Marian Reiner on behalf of the Boulder Public Library Foundation, Inc.

"Jump or Jiggle" by Everlyn Beyer, from ANOTHER HERE AND NOW STORY BOOK by Lucy Sprague Mitchell, copyright 1937 by E. P. Dutton, renewed © 1965 by Lucy Sprague Mitchell. Used by permission of Dutton Children's Books, A Division of Penguin Young Readers Group, A Member of Penguin Group (USA) Inc., 345 Hudson Street, New York, NY 10014. All rights reserved.

"Jilliky Jolliky" and "Rumpitty Tumpitty" © 1986 by Jack Prelutsky. Used by permission of HarperCollins Publishers.

"You Are My Sunshine," by Jimmie Davis. © 1940 by Peer International Corporation. Copyright Renewed. International Copyright Secured. Used by Permission. All Rights Reserved.

"Happy Birthday to You." Words and music by Mildred J. Hill and Patty S. Hill. © 1935 (Renewed) Summy-Birchard Company. All Rights Reserved. Used by Permission of Alfred Publishing Co. Inc.

"How Turtles Got Their Shells", adapted with permission from Joseph Bruchac, "How Turtle Flew South for the Winter (or, Why Turtle Has a Cracked Shell)," a story from *Native American Stories,* Told by Joseph Bruchac © 1991. By permission of Fulcrum Publishing.

ILLUSTRATION AND PHOTO CREDITS

Every effort has been taken to trace and acknowledge copyrights. The editors tender their apologies for any accidental infringement where copyright has proved untraceable. They would be pleased to insert the appropriate acknowledgment in any subsequent edition of this book. Trademarks and trade names are shown in this book for illustrative purposes only and are the property of their respective owners. The references to trademarks and trade names given herein do not affect their validity.

Art Resource, NY: 166, 175

Lina Chesak-Liberace: 32-50

Bettmann/CORBIS: 106, 109

Bridgeman Art Library/Getty Images: 105

CORBIS: xii, 114-115, 121, 122 top, 123, 127 bottom right, 130, 139, 143 right, 150, 152, 155, 163 top, 164, 171 top, 177 top

Getty Images: 109, 113 bottom, 116 bottom, 117, 119-120, 124, 126, 127 top and bottom left, 128-129, 131-134, 137-138, 140-142, 143 left, 144, 146-149, 154, 156-162, 163 bottom, 180, 184, 188, 194

Barbara L. Gibson: 135-136, 145, 151, 153

Hutton Archive/Getty Images: 104

Kunstmuseum Basel: 172

Erich Lessing/Art Resource, NY: 176

Library of Congress: 122 bottom

W. L. McCoy: 118

G. B. McIntosh: 52-102, 110-112

The Metropolitan Museum of Art, Gift of Edward S. Harkness, 1917 (17.9.1). Photograph © 1992 The Metropolitan Museum of Art: 177 bottom

Milwaukee Art Museum: 168

Museum of the City of New York/CORBIS: 107

Museum of Fine Arts, Boston: 113 top

North Wind Picture Archives: 108

The Philadelphia Museum of Art/Art Resource, NY: 166

The Phillips Collection: 169

Rehs Galleries, Inc.: 167

Scala/Art Resource, NY. Digital image © The Museum of Modern Art: 173

Tate Gallery, London/Art Resource, NY: 171

Amy Wummer: 6-30